Ah! Mischief
The Writer and Television

Ah! Mischief
The Writer and Television

David Edgar, Trevor Griffiths,
David Hare, Julian Mitchell,
Peter Prince, Howard Schuman,
Hugh Whitemore

faber and faber

First published in 1982
by Faber and Faber Limited
3 Queen Square London WC1N 3AU
Printed in Great Britain by
Redwood Burn Ltd Trowbridge Wiltshire

British Library Cataloguing in Publication Data

Ah! mischief: the writer and television
1. Television plays—Addresses, essays,
lectures   2. Television authorship—Addresses,
essays, lectures
I. Edgar, David
808.2′2   PN1992.7

ISBN 0–571–11881–X

Contents

Publisher's Note

The audiences for television drama dwarf into statistical insignificance those for the older-established forms of live theatre or the literary novel, and yet when it comes to the amount of serious writing about it the proportions are reversed, even when the practitioners involved are the same people. In an attempt to counter this tendency, and as a contribution to the increasing but still inadequate amount of public debate, we approached several writers, many of them with experience and reputations not exclusively derived from their work in television, offering them a platform to use as they chose. This book is the result; a stimulating mix of passionate and dispassionate, objective and subjective, comment and argument on the satisfactions and frustrations of working in the medium.

The writers are: David Edgar, Trevor Griffiths, David Hare, Julian Mitchell, Peter Prince, Howard Schuman and Hugh Whitemore.

David Hare kindly agreed to let us use his title.

About the Contributors

DAVID EDGAR was born in 1948 in Birmingham. After a short career in journalism, he took up full-time writing in 1972. Since then he has written extensively for the theatre, television and radio. His past work includes *Dick Deterred* (1974), *Blood Sports* (1976), *Wreckers* (1977) and *Mary Barnes* (1978). His adaptation of *The Jail Diary of Albie Sachs* was produced in 1978 by the Royal Shakespeare Company, which also presented his award-winning play *Destiny* (1977) and his adaptation of *Nicholas Nickleby*. His television work includes versions of *Destiny* (1978) and *Jail Diary* (1980).

TREVOR GRIFFITHS was born in 1935 in Manchester. He began writing in the late 1960s after working for two years with the Further Education Department of the BBC in Manchester. His stage plays include *The Wages of Thin* (1969), *Occupations* (1970), *Sam Sam* (1972), *The Party* (1973) and *Comedians* (1975), which was later produced for television by its original director, Richard Eyre, as was his translation of Chekhov's *The Cherry Orchard* (1977). Griffiths's writing for television had included seventeen episodes of *Adam Smith* (written under the pseudonym Ben Rae) before he contributed an episode of the series *Fall of Eagles* entitled *Absolute Beginners* in 1974. This was followed by *All Good Men* (1974), *Through the Night* (1975) and *Bill Brand* (1976). He also adapted D. H. Lawrence's *Sons and Lovers* for ATV, although the series was finally produced by the BBC (1980). *Country*, his film for television, directed by Richard Eyre, was transmitted on 20 October 1981.

DAVID HARE was born in 1947 and educated at Lancing College and Jesus College, Cambridge. In 1968 he founded the Portable Theatre; from 1969 to 1971 he was the Literary Manager and Resident Dramatist at the Royal Court Theatre; and in 1973 was the Resident Dramatist at the Nottingham Playhouse. In 1975 he founded the Joint Stock Theatre Group. He is the author of the following plays: *Slag, The Great Exhibition, Knuckle, Fanshen, Teeth 'n' Smiles, Plenty*

About the Contributors

and *Map of the World* (performed at the Adelaide Festival in March 1982). His films for television include *Licking Hitler* and *Dreams of Leaving*.

JULIAN MITCHELL, born in 1935, was educated at Winchester and Wadham College, Oxford. He is a Governor of the Chelsea School of Art and from 1966 to 1969 was a Member of the Arts Council Literature Panel. In 1965 he was awarded the John Llewellyn Rhys Prize, in 1966 the Somerset Maugham Award, in 1977 the International Critics Prize in Monte Carlo, and in 1979 the John Florio Prize. He is the author of six novels, a biography of Lady Randolph Churchill, a translation of Pirandello's *Henry IV* and a number of stage plays including *Half-Life* and *Another Country*. His plays for television include *Abide With Me, A Question of Degree, The Good Soldier, Jennie, Rust, Shadow in the Sun, Staying On* and *The Mysterious Stranger*.

PETER PRINCE was born in England in 1942 and educated here and in the USA. His writing career began with the publication of a first novel, *Play Things*, which won the Somerset Maugham Award for 1973. His television career began in the same year with a Play for Today, *The Floater*, directed by Barry Davis, who also directed his most recently shown work, the *Oppenheimer* series, which won a BAFTA Award in 1981. In between there were four films for television, *Early Struggles, Play Things, Last Summer* and *Cold Harbour*, all directed by Stephen Frears. His latest TV play is *Bright Eyes*, directed by Peter Duffell, which is due for showing in the BBC's Plays for Tomorrow series in early 1982. He is currently working on a novel.

In 1980, after announcing in a *Time Out* interview that he had 'no interest in or understanding of the theatre', he settled down to write a stage play, *Television Times*, which was premiered at the RSC Warehouse at the end of that year.

HOWARD SCHUMAN was born in Brooklyn, New York, in 1942. He studied political science and theatre at Brandeis University and then undertook postgraduate work at the University of California, Berkeley, on a political science fellowship. He returned to New York, where he worked in the theatre, writing lyrics, sketches and plays for summer stock, cabaret and the fringe. He adapted Studs

12

Terkel's *Division Street America* for an experimental season at the Lincoln Center and co-authored an off-beat musical called *Up Eden*, which flopped in New York. He moved to London in 1968.

HUGH WHITEMORE was born in 1936. He is the author of many television plays and has also written extensively for the cinema, both in London and in Hollywood. He received Writers' Guild Awards for his dramatization of *Cider with Rosie* (1971) and for his contribution to Granada's celebrated *Country Matters* series (1972). With director Franc Roddam, he created the controversial drama/documentary, *Dummy*, which won the RAI Prize in the 1979 Prix Italia. His first play for the stage was *Stevie*, which was produced at the Vaudeville Theatre in 1977, with Glenda Jackson in the title role. The subsequent film version enjoyed a phenomenal success in New York.

Hugh Whitemore's latest work for television is a four-part historical drama, *I Remember Nelson*, and three adaptations for Granada's anthology series *All For Love*. He has written the screenplay for the forthcoming Alan Bridges film *The Return of the Soldier*, which stars Julie Christie, Glenda Jackson, Ann-Margret and Alan Bates.

JOHN WYVER was born in 1955. After leaving Magdalen College, Oxford, in 1977, he joined *Time Out* magazine as its television editor. During the industrial dispute there in 1981 he was a member of the chapel that founded *City Limits*. He has written about television for a wide range of journals, including the *Guardian* and *Screen*, and has organized television retrospectives at the National Film Theatre and the Institute of Contemporary Arts. In 1980 the column that he edited was awarded the Philips Media Trophy for television journalism. He is currently engaged in writing a production study of a forthcoming Wagner television series.

On Drama Documentary*

DAVID EDGAR

It's a truism that the one-off, original television play is always an endangered species; the irony of the early eighties is that the target has shifted. The most poisonous darts are now aimed not so much at the 'obscure' Second City First or the 'obscene' Play for Today, but at manifestations of the only single-play television form that is unique to the medium: the form known variously as faction, dramatic reconstruction, documentary drama or drama-documentary. This form has always had its critics, of course: Mrs Mary Whitehouse cut her teeth on *Cathy Come Home* and *Up the Junction*. But the debate over Anthony Thomas's *Death of a Princess* took matters on to a different plane. This was partly, of course, to do with the perceived threat to our trading and diplomatic links with Saudi Arabia, and most interesting it was, to see how those Conservatives who fervently believe in freedom of trade as a precondition of freedom of expression tend to support the former over the latter when the two conflict. But the importance of the affair to the makers of drama-documentary was that the film provoked many critics to express their strong reservations not just about *Death of a Princess,* but about the form as a whole.

Two extremely distinguished commentators expressed their reservations good and early: immediately after the Saudi storm broke, Sir Ian Gilmour, then the Lord Privy Seal, told the House of Commons that 'the so-called dramatization or fictionalization of alleged history is extremely dangerous and misleading, and is something to which the broadcasting authorities must give close attention.' His view was echoed by Lord Carrington in the Lords, who warned that 'it might be as well for those who are producing these programmes to have a good look at the consequences of what they are doing' (he was responding to a question about 'the tendency of some TV companies

---

* This article is a rewritten and extended version of a talk, *Acting out Facts,* broadcast on Radio Three on 28 December 1980. The talk was subsequently published, in edited forms, in the *Listener* and the *Stage.*

to present programmes deliberately designed to give the impression of documentary based on fact'). Others quickly entered the lists as well; reasonably representative were Geoffrey Cannon, writing in the *Sunday Times* (13 April 1980), and Richard Gott in the *Guardian* (6 August 1980). Cannon's basic argument against drama-documentary was that the 'known facts' of contemporary or recent history can and are subject to 'elaboration and embroidery', and, indeed, that 'TV drama-documentary may deliberately stray away from truth for dramatic impact, and to feed the audience's predispositions or prejudices.' Richard Gott's article began as follows:

Well, what is it? Fact or fiction? History or current affairs? Scarcely a night goes by nowadays without Edward the Eighth, the Reverend Jim Jones, Winston Churchill, or some other famous or infamous figure from the recent past, appearing on the television screen. Significant episodes in their lives are then presented in fictitious form ('artificial, counterfeit, sham'), or, rather, in a mishmash of fact and fiction and producer's whim. It is a profoundly unsatisfactory development in the use of television.

Gott then went on to accuse television producers and writers of usurping the function of historians, claiming to explain 'what actually happened' in history, a role for which they are neither qualified nor competent, rather than pursuing their proper role of 'illuminating the human condition' through the creation of imaginary characters in invented situations.

These are serious arguments, which deserve to be taken seriously. They are, however, based on severe misconceptions about history itself and the playwrights' relationship to it; and I use the word 'playwright' rather than producer or director deliberately, because it is my view that drama-documentary is, primarily, not a journalistic but a dramatic medium, like soap-opera, tragedy or farce, which has been developed by writers in response to the changing world about them, and that it should be defended as such.

The first and glaring problem with Gott and Cannon's critiques of the form is one of definition. Richard Gott, for example, confines himself to the discussion of plays which present the actions of famous or infamous real people, living in the recent past, in fictional form. This definition would indeed take in most of the programmes which we would recognize as drama-documentary, but it would also encompass almost any biographical film set in the recent past, from

15

David Edgar

Lawrence of Arabia and *The Dambusters* to *Funny Girl*. Geoffrey Cannon divides the form into two, distinguishing between faction (of which he gives *Roots, Holocaust* and *Washington behind Closed Doors* as examples), and drama-documentary, which he describes as a form dealing with 'matters of social and moral concern'. It is obvious that the latter definition could happily embrace almost every serious play ever written; but even the former group of plays have in common only that they deal with real historical events and use a mix of real and fictional characters—which might just about let out *Funny Girl*, if we define 'historical event' in a way that excludes the Ziegfeld Follies, but would include most biographical war films and stage plays as various as Brecht's *Galileo*, Rattigan's *The Winslow Boy* and Shaw's *Saint Joan*. And a third commentator, Robin Sutch, replying to Gott's piece in the *Guardian* (26 August 1980), went so far as to give the historical plays of Shakespeare and Aeschylus as examples of ancient precedents of the drama-documentary form. And it's worth pointing out that apart from Cannon's subjects of social and moral concern, none of the above definitions would cover programmes that most people would instinctively view as being drama-documentaries, but which do not include real people as characters, like *Law and Order*, two of the four episodes of Ken Loach's *Days of Hope*, and, indeed, *Cathy Come Home*.

It is of course true that drama-documentary makers themselves have extreme difficulty in defining the beast they are riding. But it is also clear that the above definitions won't do, and that pointing out that they won't do is more than a debating trick, because no definition of the difference between, say, *Churchill and the Generals*, *Three Days in Szczecin*, *Colditz* and *Henry V will* do unless it takes into account the dramatic and ideological purposes of playwrights, and the artistic and social contexts in which they work.

It seems to me obvious that, however inspirational the process of literary creation may be, most playwrights draw most of their subject-matter from sources outside themselves, and when critics like Richard Gott complain that by re-creating historical figures rather than creating imaginary characters writers are displaying a lack of creativity and imagination, they are themselves displaying not a little ignorance about the process of making plays. It is, however, clear why this misunderstanding occurs; it is to do with the differences between writing plays about public and private life. When playwrights write about a private theme—about, say, domestic life or

16

romantic love—their models in real life are cloaked in anonymity; the real families or couples on which the play is based are unlikely to be known to its audience. If, however, a playwright chose to write about a battle, it is likely that an intelligent audience would pick up pretty quickly whether the story was based on the Peloponnesian Wars, the Battle of Trafalgar or the Siege of Leningrad. Put another way, it is a shocking but true fact that, in France alone, literally millions of love affairs were commenced, enjoyed and concluded between 1958 and 1969, and the playwright interested in the sexual habits of the French during the first decade of the Fifth Republic would be able to base his plot on any number of them. The source material for a play about political leadership in France during that period is more limited, and it would be a perverse writer who did not consider including, in such a play, a tall, long-nosed statesman with a marked distaste for Anglo-Saxon countries and a liking for grandiose political rhetoric. And similarly, if I wanted—and as it happens, I once did—to write a play about electoral malpractice in a large English-speaking democratic state possessed of sophisticated surveillance technologies, it would be pretty coy not to set that play in Washington DC during the Nixon presidency. It is true, of course, that some plays about public life have created their own allegorical world, or used an incident from the past to illumine the present (Max Frisch's *Andorra* is an example of the former technique, Arthur Miller's *The Crucible* of the latter). But by and large plays about public life have tended to be based on real and recognizable public events, either contemporary or historical. What sets drama-documentary apart from the mass of public plays is not the employment of facts but the theatrical use to which those facts are put. In drama-documentary, I believe, the factual basis of the story gives the action of the play its credibility.

Most good plays say things about human relationships and human society which are challenging and surprising and disturbing to their audiences; and all writers of such plays want to convince their audiences that they are right to be so challenged, surprised and disturbed. Sometimes—in absurdist or symbolic drama—the power of a playwright's metaphor will be proof enough that his or her bleak (or euphoric) view of the universe is credible. But, for most of us, it is necessary to establish a bedrock of material (or a dramatic style) which is recognizable to the audience, and gives what follows its legitimacy. For example, John Hopkins's classic quartet of television plays, *Talking to a Stranger*, presented an unwelcomely bitter view of family life. What gave those plays their power—to shock and to convince—was that the characters' day-to-day behaviour was terrifyingly recognizable, when set against our own lives and the lives of people we know. In the same way, Eugene O'Neill's *Long Day's Journey into Night* is incomparably superior in its perception, its power and its capacity to disturb to anything O'Neill had written before, precisely because the desperate and magnificent agony of the Tyrones is shown to us, initially at least, through the most trivial (but universal) of domestic conflicts: over meal-times, table-clearing and drinks before dinner. Similarly, the conclusions of the plays of Shakespeare are often more radical and challenging to our assumptions about the world than anything written before or since. But the fact that Shakespeare's plays employed recognizable forms— tragedy, comedy, historical drama—provided a bedrock of shared assumptions on which he could build his vision of the human condition. Without that bedrock, that sense that the writer has won his or her spurs, the audience can shrug off the playwright's conclusions as bearing no relationship to the real world.

Playwrights writing about public life in the contemporary world are in a different position both from the writer of domestic drama and from Shakespeare. We all have experience of the subject-matter of domestic drama—we have all lived in families, grown up, fallen in love, and fallen out of it again; we can all judge our own experience against plays which present these activities to us. In public plays, however, there is no guarantee of any shared experience of the subject-matter. Plays about war are presented on British stages and British television to audiences who now, by and large, have no knowledge of soldiering. Plays about the workings of one particular political party will be performed or broadcast to audiences consisting, in varying and unpredictable proportions, of members of that party, members of opposing parties, or members of no party at all. Further, there are no longer any dramatic forms that retain the universally accepted power of, say, tragedy or the historical epic. And, of course, we live in an age in which any unifying belief or set of values—which means any generally accepted set of criteria for judging human behaviour—are absent.

I think that the theatre of fact, the documentary theatre, was created to give credibility to the playwright's analysis of the incredible happenings of our time. (The theatrical form of drama-documentary pre-dated the television form, but, in my view, it is on television that the form has reached maturity.) One of the best examples of stage drama-documentary is Rolf Hochhuth's play *The Representative,* written in the early 1960s. Hochhuth wanted to write a play about men of power, and the terrible contradiction they face in balancing political expediency against moral principle. He decided to set his play not in the far or mythical past, but during the Second World War. The context of the play's story—the Holocaust—was then and is now well known. But Hochhuth's central incident—the refusal of Pope Pius XII to break the Vatican's Concordat with the Third Reich in protest against the mass-murder of the Jews—was not well known at all, and Hochhuth's representation of the Pope's actions provoked bitter controversy when the play was first staged. It's my belief that Hochhuth's statement on the Holocaust and the resistance to it would not have been nearly so powerful if it had not exposed an event of history about which his audience knew little or nothing. His act of documentary revelation performed, in his play, an equivalent function to that of the peripeteia of Greek tragedy: the sudden, unexpected and shocking reversal of fortune that captures and freezes the themes of the play, as if caught in a sudden shaft of bright light. The scene with the Pope in *The Representative* is in fact a reversal of *expectation,* both about the character and about the type of play we are watching; and the credibility it gives to Hochhuth's message is not about the following of agreed and accepted constructional rules, but about evidence.

This is a completely different use of historical fact in drama from, for example, that of Shakespeare in his history plays. Shakespeare drew stories from a variety of sources to explore the theme of kingship, including ancient Roman, recent British and mythological history. I don't believe, however, that the fact that the plots of *King Lear* and *Macbeth* were drawn from mythology, and those of *Henry VI* and *Richard II* from relatively recent history, makes Shakespeare's use of his source material substantially different. In all these cases he was writing tragedies; in no case was he revealing anything his audience couldn't have known. In one case, *Richard III*, he made a play of great dramatic power out of a set of facts that were almost certainly completely untrue.

In contrast, documentary drama relies on its facts being correct. The moral core of Rolf Hochhuth's second play (*Soldiers,* a critique of allied civilian bombing in the war) was undermined and destroyed by the historical *un*truth of an important though secondary incident in the play. Similarly, the power of *Cathy Come Home* depended on the fact that its thesis—that British cities suffered from wretchedly inadequate housing at a time of presumed general prosperity—was timely and true. Without that fact, *Cathy* would have been little more than a sad anecdote of an inadequate family destroyed by an indifferent bureaucracy. In reality, of course, the play changed the way we think about housing. I think it changed the way we think about other things too—like the inner-city, the role of the social services, and even the political system. Jeremy Sandford used his factual base in order to give dramatic force and credibility to a much wider theme.

It is of course precisely this *use* of factual material to sustain a thesis which provokes so much concern and criticism. As Leslie Woodhead of Granada Television's drama-documentary unit argued in his Granada lecture (BFI, 19 May 1981), 'the underlying assumption that television drama should seek not only to reflect but also to change society has informed much of the most interesting work in the field of documented drama over the past decade', citing the work of Tony Garnett, Ken Loach, Jim Allen and G. F. Newman, and pointing out that 'the implied worry . . . is that the forms and credibilities of documentary and news are being recruited to smuggle a political message.' Certainly this worried Paul Johnson, in a piece commenting on *World in Action*'s reconstruction of the Cabinet debate over the 1981 budget (the *Listener,* 19 March 1981): for him, drama-documentary deliberately blurs the fact/fiction distinction 'for tendentious purposes, often in pursuit of partisan political ends . . . The object, quite brazenly, is to influence opinion on contentious matters.' The same point was made by Geoffrey Cannon in his post-*Princess* piece in the *Sunday Times:*

> What I found disturbing about Ian Curteis's two recent dramatized reconstructions *Churchill and the Generals* and *Suez 1956* was that, in both cases, Curteis—as he stated openly and honestly—had a thesis about Churchill and about Eden (put simply, that they were liable to states of mind approaching dementia) and he used known facts to demonstrate his thesis. . . . And while his thesis is—as far as I know—consistent with the facts, other interpretations are equally consistent.

The problems with these arguments are several-fold. While few people would justify the deliberate falsification or invention of incidents to support a vacuous historical argument (it is right that the film *The Deer Hunter* was criticized for apparently inventing its central metaphor of a group of Vietcong guerrillas forcing their American captors to play Russian roulette), accusations of political bias have a tendency to be oddly selective (no problems, as Ken Loach points out, 'when Edward VII or Churchill's mother are romanticized and glorified'). Further, as Leslie Woodhead argues, even the makers of 'real' current affairs and news programmes are at last owning up about 'the inescapable subjective content in every camera movement and edit', and the fact that 'the manipulative presence of the director is as significant in *Johnny Go Home* as it was in *Cathy Come Home.*' But even more interesting, from the dramatist's point of view, is Richard Gott's unflattering comparison between the 'amateur' writer of drama-documentary and the professional historian.

In his witty and wonderful book *What is History?*,* Professor E. H. Carr takes much pleasure in exposing the nineteenth-century view of history as a collection of objective facts that it is the historian's task merely to discover, separate from speculation, and reveal. In reality, as Carr points out, it is a subjective value-judgement that Caesar's crossing of the Rubicon is an important historical event, but that the fact that millions of other people have and still do cross that petty stream—in both directions and for reasons doubtless important for them—is not a matter of any historical importance. Similarly, almost all our knowledge of Greece in the period of the Persian Wars is not objective knowledge at all, because it emanates exclusively from a small group of rich people in the one city of Athens. Further, our view that the medieval period was a time of great religious commitment might well have been influenced by the fact that almost all the contemporary chroniclers of that period were monks. And, finally, even those documents precisely designed to be pragmatically factual—minutes of meetings and so on—reflect the interests and prejudices and self-view of the person by whom or for whom the documents were written. Professor Carr gives the example of the papers of Gustav Stresemann, the Foreign Minister of the Weimar Republic, which were published after his death in 1929 in three massive volumes, which concentrate almost entirely on Stresemann's successful diplomatic dealings with the West. This, as Carr points out, itself distorts history, as Stresemann in fact devoted a lot, even a majority, of his time to the pursuit of a much less successful policy

* Published by Penguin Books, Harmondsworth, 1964.

towards the Soviet Union. But the point is that, even if the published selection were complete or accurately represented the whole, then the minutes of Stresemann's meetings with, say, the Soviet Foreign Minister Chicherin would tell us not what actually happened, but only what Stresemann thought had happened, or what he wanted others to think, or wanted himself to think, or (most likely of all) what his secretary felt that he might want to think had happened. And Chicherin's records of the same conversation would doubtless look very different, but they would be strikingly similar in one respect: they would be highly contentious, tendentious, and politically partisan.

But it is useful to take this example even further. Suppose, which is not the case, that historians had available to them both sets of minutes, Stresemann's and Chicherin's. I suspect—and I only suspect, because I'm not a historian—that they would look at those two accounts in two ways. First, the historian would set them against other facts, and if, for example, it was found that either statesman had said something he knew to be untrue, then he or she might conclude that the person was being either cunning, devious, or at least excessively cautious with the other. Second, the historian might set the documents against what could be discovered about the characters of the two men from other sources; what their relatives, friends and acquaintances said about them. What I suspect the historian would not do—because it would be a most unscholarly procedure— would be to set the recollections of these two men of this one event against the behaviour of the historian's *own* relatives, friends or aquaintances, or, even, against the behaviour of him or herself. It is *that* knowledge, knowledge not just of human behaviour but of the skills necessary to communicate that knowledge to others, which is the treasured possession of the creators of dramatic fiction. They do it all the time. And, in particular, they have throughout the ages developed ways of showing the kind of behaviour that tends to occur at meetings between the representatives of suspicious and hostile countries; of demonstrating the gap between what people say, and what they mean, and what they subsequently do. A historian can say, of course, and back up the assertion, that a king claimed to be wise, just and merciful when he was actually engaged in bumping off all his opponents. But only a dramatist can demonstrate how that hypocrisy manifests itself in the human soul: the self-deception, the paranoia, even the glorification of deceit, that go on in the minds of men and women whose public and private faces are at war. (And in this context, I have always thought it significant that the soliloquy and the aside have been such enduring devices in the playwright's armoury; they are, of course, devices precisely designed to show the gap between what someone says and what they think and feel.)

What I am saying is that dramatic fiction can uniquely illumine certain aspects of public life; and the dramatic power of drama-documentary lies in its capacity to show us not that certain events occurred (the headlines can do that) or even, perhaps, why they occurred (for such information we can go to the weekly magazines or the history books), but *how* they occurred: how recognizable human beings rule, fight, judge, meet, negotiate, suppress and overthrow. Perhaps the simplest example of the achievement of such an effect is in the actual physical reconstruction of a public event: trials, for example, can be comprehensively reported, but nobody who watched, say, the reconstructions of the *Gay News* blasphemy case, or the Chicago Conspiracy hearings, could fail to take away from those experiences not merely a richer sense of atmosphere, but a profounder understanding of the processes by which men and women advocate, defend themselves, give evidence and pass judgement. There are many other public processes ripe for such treatment: I have recently been involved (for the first time) in trade union negotiations, and was deeply impressed by the gap between the public image of such events and the reality. I am sure that when negotiators have behind them millions or thousands of manual workers (as opposed to our couple of hundred stage-playwrights) matters feel a little different; but I'm equally sure that all negotiations ultimately come down to spatial relationships, the time of day, the length and structure of the meeting, and basic states of mind like tiredness, irritation and impatience (on the one hand), and confidence, bloody-mindedness and a functioning sense of humour (on the other).

The group of drama-documentary makers to have applied such principles to their craft with most consistency and rigour have been the Manchester-based Granada unit, under Leslie Woodhead. In one sense it is somewhat paradoxical that this group should have sought to apply what are (I have argued) essentially dramatic criteria to their work, because, as Woodhead explained in his Granada lecture (quoted above), he entered the field at precisely the opposite corner:

My own motive for taking up the drama-documentary trade was

23

simple, pragmatic, and, I suspect, to some degree representative. As a television journalist working on *World in Action*, I came across an important story I wanted to tell, but found there was no other way to tell it. The story was about a Soviet dissident imprisoned in a mental hospital. By its very nature, it was totally inaccessible by conventional documentary methods. But the dissident, General Grigorenko, had managed to smuggle out of mental prison a detailed diary of his experiences. As a result, it was possible to produce a valid dramatic reconstruction of what happened to Grigorenko and tell that important story.... The basic impulse behind the drama-documentary form is, I suggest, simply to tell to a mass audience a real and relevant story involving real people. The basic problem is how to get it right after the event.

For Woodhead, the priorities have remained 'obstinately journalistic', with an emphasis on exhaustive research and cross-checking, 'and on high-grade source material such as tape-recordings and transcripts'. But I would argue that the *results* of Woodhead's painstaking work have been increasingly dramatic, in the technical sense of that word. In the Grigorenko drama-documentary (titled *The Man Who Wouldn't Keep Quiet*, and scripted by Woodhead himself in 1970), the 'dramatic' element of the production consisted (by and large) of visual evocations of Grigorenko's protests, arrests, trials and incarcerations; hardly a word (apart from an explanatory commentary) did not originate in Grigorenko's own diary. In Granada's second drama-documentary treatment of East European resistance (*Three Days in Szczecin*, scripted by Boleslaw Sulik and broadcast in 1976), the main action (the historical meeting between Polish Party leader Gierek with striking shipbuilders in 1971) was based on an actual tape-recording of the proceedings, but was amplified and fleshed-out by the memories of strike leader Edmund Baluka (by then an exile in England). Baluka's reminiscences (as an openly acknowledged source) allowed Sulik and Woodhead to go much further in re-creating not just the facts of what was said and who said it, but how the listeners reacted, inside and outside the meeting hall. *Three Days* was indeed a remarkable representation of an extraordinary historical event; it was also a peculiarly authoritative play about how meetings occur.

Woodhead's most recent drama-documentary (at the time of writing a further treatment of Polish worker resistance was being planned for broadcast at the end of 1981) was *Invasion*, scripted by David Boulton and shown in 1980. The programme fitted neatly into Granada's drama-documentary criteria: it showed events (surrounding the Soviet invasion of Czechoslovakia) which could only be reconstructed; it was based on rigorous research. But for the viewer it was a play, in which recognizable human beings negotiated, discussed, argued, lost their tempers, kept their cool, supported and betrayed each other. Two examples may suffice: at one point in the play, a friend sends in beer and sandwiches for the Czech Politburo, by now effectively imprisoned by the Soviet invaders. After several moments of agonizing indecision, the Czechs choose to offer part of their meal to the nervously polite Russian soldiers guarding them. Similarly, later on, another imprisoned Czech leader discovers that he and his Polish guard were members of the same unit of the International Brigade in Spain, and they swap reminiscences until the irony of the situation becomes too much for them. These are not just anecdotes, bits of what journalists call 'colour'. They may not be the usual stuff of historical scholarship, but they are absolutely the stuff of history.

No one would argue, however, least of all David Boulton, that his play was impartial. It was written from the point of view of the liberals on the Czech central committee, and doubtless the conservatives in the Soviet leadership would regard these events in a very different light. Further, the play was largely based on the recollections of one person: Zdenek Mlynar, part-author of the Action Programme of the Prague Spring. But, again, the programme makers were completely honest about this fact, and Boulton began his play with a shot of the real Mlynar, standing next to the actor playing him, on the Austro-Czech border, and reiterated the point frequently by using Mlynar's own recollections, in the past tense, as a commentary on the action. The viewers were therefore completely aware of the perspective from which the events were being seen; they could judge, for instance, Boulton's dramatization of Mlynar's initial refusal, and subsequent agreement, to sign the Soviet-drafted communiqué that sold out the Prague Spring, against the fact that the scene was based on Mlynar's own recollections.

E. H. Carr argues that, in reality, the historian is a kind of protagonist in the history he or she is writing. In *Invasion*, the protagonist was Mlynar, with a little help from David Boulton. In other plays, however, the playwright him or herself becomes a central character.

David Edgar

As I have pointed out, the writer Ian Curteis has been particularly berated for his treatment of Churchill and Eden; Geoffrey Cannon was concerned that 'millions of viewers will continue to see Churchill and Eden through Ian Curteis's eyes.' Now, I am sure that Curteis (who always insists that his works are firmly labelled as plays rather than drama-documentaries) feels that he has found the truth about his subjects, and hopes that others will agree with him. I'm not sure that I do, but I *am* sure that I find Curteis's vision revealing about both his and our attitudes, in our own time, towards these two important figures in our national mythology; in the same way as I find the novels of Evelyn Waugh perceptive, although I am not a High Tory, and the plays of Bernard Shaw instructive, although I am not a Fabian either. But the important point is that, like David Boulton, Ian Curteis writes plays, in which people are shown doing things that human beings do, and we are able to judge the quality of the writer's vision by the simple method that we unconsciously employ whenever we watch a piece of dramatic fiction—by asking the basic question as to whether it is credible that people should behave like this, setting what we see against our own experience of human affairs. And in the case of Curteis there are two bonuses: we have our own knowledge or even experience of the Suez crisis and the Second World War as yardsticks, and we can also judge Curteis's Eden and Churchill against other dramatic representations of the two men on stage and screen. With that armoury of weapons of judgement, one may respectfully suggest that if viewers do indeed continue to see the two statesmen through Ian Curteis's eyes, it is because they have judged his perception to be keener than the alternatives on offer.

And in this context, I can mention a case from my own experience. I can, perhaps, lay claim to having been the writer of the purest drama-documentary ever written, because, in 1974, during the Watergate crisis, I edited the White House tape transcripts into a forty-five-minute television play, in which every word spoken on screen had been actually spoken in reality, and we had the transcripts to prove it. But, in fact, of course, the play was bristling with impurities: the whole process of making it had consisted of value-judgements, from my judgements about what to put in and leave out, to the director's judgements about what to look at, and the actors' judgements about pace and inflection and gesture and mood. And those judgements—about how the words were said, and why, and with what relative significance—added up to an argument, which was that Richard Nixon was progressively deluding himself about what he was doing, and that when he said he didn't know things that he did know, he wasn't pretending but concealing the memory from himself. And although I think we were right, it is equally possible to argue that Nixon knew exactly what he was doing, and was deceiving everybody *except* himself. But I'm sure that our act of turning those documents into drama, of showing one way in which those words *could* have been spoken by real human beings, had the effect of deepening our audience's understanding of those extraordinary events, and it may even have proved, for those who disagreed with our interpretation of the events, that they were right and we were wrong.

The threat to drama-documentary does not just consist of critical attacks from critics, pundits and Ministers of the Crown. In November 1980, the Broadcasting Act became law, and with it, the provisions for the setting up of a Broadcasting Complaints Commission came into effect. Broadcasters had been acquainted with the baleful nature of this body a few months earlier, when lawyer Geoffrey Robertson had addressed the Edinburgh Television Festival on the subject of the BCC (his address was reprinted in the *Listener*, 11 September 1980):

> In the short space of three hours, the Commons Committee on the Broadcasting Bill approved the construction of a special court to judge radio and television programmes: the Broadcasting Complaints Commission. It will comprise 'three wise men' with no media links, appointed by the Home Secretary, to 'adjudicate upon complaints of unjust or unfair treatment ... or unwarranted infringement of privacy'. Replete with a staff of 'officers and servants' paid for by a special levy on broadcasting companies, it will sit in secret to consider complaints from individuals (alive or dead), companies, clubs and foreign countries. It will summon broadcasting executives, call for correspondence, and hand down judgements which must be published in any way it directs.

Acting without even the right of appeal, the BCC has the potential of being a mighty force for censorship, particularly in the form of self-censorship before the event. As Robertson pointed out:

> The BCC, as it has emerged from this process, is no longer an exercise in accountability. It is an exercise in control. It will become another means of levering television and radio into a strait-

jacket which could never be contemplated for newspapers, books or plays. It is not an effective method for securing a 'right of reply' for persons whose actions have been distorted, and its function is far removed from the desirable end of providing a speedy correction of untruths. It is, in effect, a court, whose case law will impinge on the way television programmes are made, the nature of subject-matter selected, and the techniques used for bringing history, drama and current affairs to life on the small screen.

The implications for historical plays and drama-documentary are indeed awesome. Even after the Government amended the provision that would allow the relatives, friends and admirers of the dead to complain on their behalf (the Richard III Society?), the present procedure would allow the Saudi Government to complain about *Death of a Princess,* the Soviet leadership to demand reparation for *Invasion,* and veterans of the ATS to prevent a second showing of Ian McEwan's *The Imitation Game.* Doubtless the social service ministries would have had a high old time with *Cathy Come Home* and *Spongers* (and the Police Federation with *Law and Order*) as well.

Not surprisingly, the BCC has the support of Mrs Mary Whitehouse (in a letter to the *Listener,* 15 January 1981, and elsewhere), and the ubiquitous Paul Johnson has applauded the Commission as 'an element of salutary terror' to be wielded against the 'new breed of young, radical producers and directors, some still in their twenties, who are without scruple in their pursuit of what they believe to be higher causes' (the *Listener,* 1 January 1981).

As long ago as 1951, drama-documentary maker Caryl Doncaster stated that 'the dramatized story documentary is one of the few art forms pioneered by television.' It is important that the form be defended for that reason alone; but there are wider implications. Through all the criticisms of drama-documentary runs a single thread of assumption: that, while clever, educated people are able to recognize and judge a thesis when they see one, ordinary television viewers can somehow be duped into accepting an argument as objective fact. As it happens, the so-called cheap, popular newspapers are full of letters from people who are highly critical of television programmes that do not live up to the virtues that their makers claim for them, whether those virtues are those of entertainment or of historical truth. But even if it could be proved (and I doubt it mightily) that the majority of viewers really will take at face value anything that is pumped out at them, then it is an extraordinary indictment *not of drama-documentary*, but of the rest of television, that it is so uniform, so uncontentious and so bland that it has bludgeoned its audience into a state of passive acceptance of everything they watch.

As a writer about public life, I would defend drama-documentary as a form in which important things can be said in a uniquely authoritative and credible way. But the form also needs to be defended because the presence of drama-documentary in the schedules is an active encouragement to audiences to think critically and seriously about all the programmes they watch.

Countering Consent:
An Interview with John Wyver

TREVOR GRIFFITHS

Trevor Griffiths is a writer passionately committed both to socialism and to television. This dual commitment is best expressed by him in an extract from his 1977 preface to the published versions of *Through the Night* and *Such Impossibilities*:

> Of all the outlets available to a playwright for his work, television seems to me at once the most potent and the most difficult; the most potent and *therefore* the most difficult, one's inclined to add.... For most people (in Britain now) plays are television plays, 'drama' is television drama (though it's a word used almost exclusively by those responsible for *production*, rarely if ever by audiences). A play on television, transmitted in mid-evening on a weekday, will make some sort of contact with anything from 3 to 12 million people (20 if it's a series), usually all at the same time. And the *potential* audience, because of television's irreversibly network nature, is every sighted person in the society with a set and the time and desire to watch. Not surprisingly, a medium as potentially dangerous as this one will need to be *controlled* with some rigour and attention to detail. 'To inform' and 'to educate' may well be in the charter, alongside 'to entertain', but information that inflames and education that subverts will find its producers facing unrenewed contracts and its contributors mysteriously dropped.... It would be odd, of course, if it were otherwise. In a society predicated on the exploitation of the many by the few, in a world a large part of which operates according to precisely the same capitalist principle, yet where the necessary tactical avowal of democratic process has led to its actualization, however shallowly, and not always so, in the minds and actions of the exploited, the shaping of consciousness, the erection of the

superstructure of consent, will become the major cultural concern of the state and the dominant class or classes it represents.

All of Griffiths's work, for television, the theatre, and, recently and abortively, for the film industry, has been directed at subverting that 'shaping of consciousness'.

Can we discuss the relative merits of working on tape in the studio, and on film?

What is strong about film, as opposed to work done on videotape in the studio, is that you do it away from the institution. That means that you can keep other eyes away from it until the last possible moment. Garnett and Loach have worked marvellously in this way. *Days of Hope* is a classic example of their control of material, which is as much an ideological as a formal and technical control. Then you can choose the ground on which you have your confrontation with the funding authority.

In the studio you can't do it like that; the studio has monitors freely available to administrative and executive staff. When we were making *Adam Smith* and indeed *Occupations* at Granada, we knew that on the sixth floor people could flick from studio to studio and see . . . 'Oh they're coming up to that one, there's a bit of sex there. Well we don't want to see that breast do we, that's out.'

Is control really as crude as that?

It *can* be. Usually staff producers or Heads of Department don't like to confront the issue at the point of production. They like to get there a lot earlier than that. But you get Heads of Department who come into the gallery when difficult little scenes are being presented. We had that with *Sons and Lovers*, when Clara Dawes removes her clothes on the night after the theatre and kneels down in front of the fire. Since there was an American co-producer, the BBC felt that it had to take some account of that and asked us to reshoot it, not for home consumption but for foreign consumption. That's just one tiny example of the process.

Another occurred on *Bill Brand* when we had a meeting with the Head of Drama some days before we did a love-making scene. We were told fairly explicitly what would be allowed and what would not be allowed by the IBA: women cannot be totally naked on television in a love-making position, pubic hair will not be seen. I deliberately

31

asked, not that I'd written it, but I asked 'Well what about a rear entry penetration, is that on?' Definitely out. But not a word of that exists on paper, it's always the phone, always the chat, and a fair bit of control is exerted in that way.

What other problems have you encountered?

Well I had some serious problems with the production of *Adam Smith*. I never saw the series as about the kirk. When I did researches it was about social and political issues and that's how I conceived the series and I think that's how I wrote it. But I had no automatic right of entry into the production process and I found that many ideological insertions were being made from producers, directors and actors. So that I felt like somebody making wallpaper. I hated that but it taught me a very important lesson, which is that television is very powerful, not just as a medium of communication but as an institution, an establishment, a set of practices and relationships. I learnt that that power had to be tackled if a writer was going to do anything. For example I was away in South Africa working on the second series while members of the production team were editing Episode 13 of the first. When I got back they had taken out a huge amount of what I'd said. The final statement was a bit like a sermon on the cross; it was about a million unemployed, about social conditions, equality and justice, and they'd just hacked it to pieces. I was aghast and distraught and probably behaved very intemperately but I was mad, and though I wrote the next lot, I took my pseudonym [Ben Rae] off it and parted company with the series thereafter.

Did you try to increase the standing of your role as a writer in the production process?

I felt it was urgent that I should do that because what we were talking about was text, meanings, values. You see I didn't come into writing as an *auteur*, that is to say as a person who wanted to splash his ego around this society. Playwriting to me has always seemed an intervention, another way of getting things said and getting things done. I was not saying 'This is art, treat my art carefully.' I was saying 'How can you do that, that doesn't make sense.' If I ask for the guy to play Bartók, I don't want him to sit there listening to *Hair*— it's just silly. And those were the production values that were being inscribed into the text. It wasn't that *I'd* thought of Bartók, it was just that Bartók was such a radically different idea and it seemed to me

32

demeaning that you couldn't get an audience to see that. An audience will see it if you allow them, but if you make the change they won't. So I was asked to leave the gallery and I did have some unpleasant times with various directors. On the other hand there were some terribly good directors and I saw for the first time that it was possible to get a good relationship with a director in television.

What about your position as a writer in relation to factors seemingly outside your control? Scheduling, for example?

Well you can always push, push for information, for a good position in the evening's viewing. And you can make a noise if things happen badly, as with, for example, *Comedians*, when at the last minute they decided to lift it out of its 9.25 slot and put it on at 10.10.

But can you be effective?

Sometimes, but each time is different. I thought I had *Comedians* covered and suddenly it slipped out. The best I could do was to go to BAFTA, where they preview for the critics, and address the sleeping journalists who'd just watched the tape. Yet they control the tactics of that by telling other people, so that eventually it gets back to Richard Eyre [the director] and me as 'If only you'd taken the word "fuck" out.' I hung on and said that they knew what they were buying. I even said I'd have it edited as long as they put a whistle where the word 'fuck' should be, so that people watching would know that the BBC had taken that decision and not me. But of course they don't like censoring in the way that you insist on them censoring. So they censored it by lifting it and putting it out after 10 o'clock and denying me an audience.

Will you ever be able to build into contracts real control of all aspects of your text, including credit sequences and trails for example? Will writers ever have that industrial power?

'Contract' is an area I've been looking at increasingly over the last two years. Unfortunately it's such a bourgeois process but I've seen nothing to stop writers from saying, 'Look from the minute this opens to the minute this closes, visually and aurally, I am involved, the text is involved.' Now the last thing I want to do in my working practice is inhibit the autonomous procedures of other workers. I'm just trying to prioritize the text and I don't do it, I repeat, on grounds of ego, or for self-inflation. I do it because getting it right is the most

33

important thing there is. If you don't get it right, why are you broadcasting it, what's the point of issuing a message that's got distorted and become its opposite?

But the experience of Bill Brand *was different from the creation of most television. Is that the most collective way of working that you've experienced in the medium?*

Yes I'm quite sure it is. Something quite new was nearly born on that. We've all spun off into our own void a little since then but something very important occurred on *Bill Brand*. Partly because we were in production for so long—we were rehearsing *Bill Brand*, thinking *Bill Brand*, acting *Bill Brand*, it was *Bill Brand* and nothing else, week in and week out. We managed to gather some wisdom from what we were doing and feed it in; so it grew better and better as it developed, because of what we had learned. And there was a very collective shape to the whole enterprise.

How did that work in practice?

We had three directors, Michael Lindsay-Hogg, Roland Joffe and Stuart Burge who was also the overall producer. We were working in a package put together by the independent producer Stella Richman, which had been sold to Thames. There was conflict between the Stella Richman organization and Thames and we sheltered under that conflict, so while they were working out their problems, we were able to work out ours. And there was just extraordinary purchase on the imagination and spirit of the people who were involved. There were six or eight continuing characters of considerable weight in the texts, and these people got charged, and I have to say that many people at Thames got charged by it as well. The two designers were magnificent and just gave everything to the project, we had a great location manager, two terrific lighting men, marvellous actors. So that by the end we were a collective. Nobody laid down laws and said this is what we're going to do. Decisions were very widely shared.

Towards the end of the production there had always been the chance that we might get on in March, prime time as far as the year is concerned. I wanted a 9 o'clock showing but it turned out that Jeremy Isaacs, Programme Controller at Thames, had failed to sell it to the network like that. The network controllers thought that summer was the best time, possibly at 10.30. We put the word out and something like seventy people turned up for this meeting with

Isaacs on the rehearsal-room floor and he got a lot thrown at him. He was terrific and it was particularly difficult because he was passionate about the series. But he took an hour or so of verbal punishment and he went back and fought for 9 o'clock, which we got, in the summer. Now I've been in one or two situations in the theatre like that but never one in television. You see the actor in television is in a particularly difficult position because so much of an actor's income is dependent on favour, the nod, the wink. It means acquitting him or herself with propriety and that very often means not behaving as a worker at all. In a way they took a great risk in turning up like that.

But can that change, perhaps with the new Channel Four? Could you and a group of people work in that collective way with Channel Four?

If you're getting work through to Channel Four through ATV or one of the other established companies, then you will still have their supervention. If you're doing it direct as an independent company, who knows? The channel is still going to be controlled by the IBA and so they're still going to have very negative things to say about certain aspects of everyday life, about sexuality or politics. I'm hoping that that spirit of experimentation, that ferment which seems to be building will actualize itself and people will be prepared to take risks. Because though they may be risks in relation to their own careers, they're really risks on behalf of a viewing public, a popular audience which has been systematically denied important aspects of reality in their television drama. This is a perennial argument I've been having with Jeremy Isaacs since *Bill Brand*. But what television drama have you seen which honestly and rigorously presents or examines human sexuality? I haven't seen any. I've tried to write some and I've had it fairly ruthlessly winkled out, abused, distorted into something else. So just at that level there's a whole politics waiting to be exploded and I'm very interested to see if it will be. I hope it will and I hope that the collective will become more and more of a way to work. There's nothing like it; when you get into it everybody gets bigger.

But are the studio system and the industrial structure of television too inflexible, too resistant to that?

I don't believe so. There's something about the content of drama production that is different from the content of, say, car production.

Trevor Griffiths

That might be your recognition of it as a writer, but is it the understanding of the guy who pulls the lamps around in the studio?

I think that is a recognition that could be achieved for everybody in drama production from executive to chippie. Nor do I think that that is idealist, I think it is possible within the very texture and fabric of the industrial process of drama. We've already seen it work to some extent, on *Bill Brand* and on *Sons and Lovers*. But it has to work earlier than the production itself, it has to be part of the pre-production process. Now it is possible to get senior cameramen involved, it's possible to get vision mixers involved, at their level of technical speciality. What is much more difficult is the involvement of the electricians. Because to somebody moving a lamp around, it's moving a lamp around, and if he's just moving that lamp because his boss told him to, that's not the sort of involvement that leads to a collective enterprise. And the companies are structurally resistant to large numbers of people being involved in pre-production.

Although you've written a number of successful and distinguished theatre plays, the bulk of your time in the last fifteen years has been devoted to creating work for television.

Yes. I knew from very early on that I wanted to work on television, do television pieces. Television seemed then and still seems a massively powerful intervention, a means of intervening in society's life.

And unlike a number of your contemporaries you've been keen to work not just with that 'reputable' and 'serious' form of television, the single play or film. You've embraced opportunities to write for popular series, not only of your own creation like Bill Brand, *but also anthology series originated by producers.* Absolute Beginners *was written for the* Fall of Eagles *series and* Such Impossibilities *was commissioned, but never produced, for* The Edwardians. *Were they written with a specific strategic intention?*

With a strategic intent shaped by the opportunity. I worked very hard on both of those texts and I think a good deal of whatever makes a play good has gone into *Such Impossibilities*. I think it's a great shame that it wasn't ever done, particularly since I did watch the series, having had a piece rejected, and it seemed to me it would have fitted perfectly. In fact it's what the series needed and didn't have. But that's history.

Absolute Beginners is my most popular play, having been seen in sixty-five or seventy different countries. That was a great decision; I'm glad I had the wit to see it. What was good was that I didn't have a head cluttered with notions of high art and popular art, nor did I have a sense that my career rested in the high art direction rather than in the popular direction. I was committed to communicating across as wide a societal band as I possibly could. And I was just eager and excited to get something said that was complex and severe and entertaining.

That's been my position. The reason that I reject things, opportunities for communicating, are always to do with the production: how serious are these people, are they really going to do this properly or are they going to mess around? I had an offer four or five years ago to do a piece on Rosa Luxemburg in a series about Great Women. I'd have loved to have done that. But I began to sense that what they were after were, to a large extent, vehicles for performances. And I stopped. I have to do something seriously, in my way, and it can't be something else.

Again unlike a number of your contemporaries, all of your work exhibits a highly conscious awareness of the conventions and genres of television.

I don't have any settled view of art, or drama, which I think some people writing on the Left do, about their own work. I don't feel that there is something about 'art' which cuts through caked perceptions and ways of reading, seeing, feeling and thinking, and gets to the essence—I think that whole idea is nonsense. The plays which get deepest are plays which are aware of their own conventions, or other conventions, and which somehow or other manage to spring the unexpected within those conventions. I hope *Country* will work in this way. Its whole relationship to genre is very important, more important than in any other of my plays, with the possible exception of *Bill Brand* where the genre is the television serial.

But you've also reworked the hospital series in Through the Night. *And reworked the classic serialization with* Sons and Lovers, *taking a revered author like Lawrence and rethinking him in a very radical way.*

It may be that that's the way I work. But *Country* might be some steps ahead of all that, in its reflexivity, its ability to calculate that critical distance. Which is a felt and feelable relationship between what I'm doing and what has been done before.

37

Trevor Griffiths

One aspect of that is Country's *relationship to* The Godfather, *to that kind of dynastic saga. The family, for example, is called Carlion, one sound away from Corleone.*

There is a highly conscious shaping going on which was nowhere near as conscious, for example, in *Through the Night*. I knew that I had to take on the idea of the hospital as a television fact when I wrote it, but I didn't consciously seek the devices for achieving that. I suppose that was because the matter was so hot, I was writing it in the shadow of my wife's mastectomy, and the very difficult relationship which had preceded it. So the relationship to genre was a less urgent component of that. Here, in *Country*, it might almost have achieved an elegance; I'm almost embarrassed by it.

The most obvious difference between Country *and your earlier work is the absence of the lengthy arguments, the speeches, the explicit thought, so apparent in, say,* The Party *and* Occupations.

That's true. The text was written very much as a film. A tremendous amount of learning took place in the two recent years when I was in and out of Hollywood and I think that I have made a significant technical and formal advance in this text. I've managed to concentrate meaning visually and gesturally and return to movement. That has been a move away from the lengthy, articulated ratiocination which is one way, a rather dumb way, of characterizing my earlier plays. But that sounds as if it's form learning from form and I don't think that's the case.

There's something about the content of *Country* which forces a different way of working and a different way of perceiving. It's because I had no emphatic remembered experience to share with the upper class that I had to find a way of seeing them that was at one and the same time both realistic and set at a considerable critical distance. So that's the form, that I hope is what we've achieved in the production—the sense of life being lived, real space being occupied, and yet a cool, detached but mobile camera seeing them from another point of view than their own.

Most of your work has been firmly within the realistic mode.

Well I have worked in non-realistic, post-realistic areas. I did a television play with Snoo Wilson in 1975 called *Don't Make Waves*. It was a sort of state of England play, and I say that ironically because it was a farce. It was set in the aftermath of a mysterious explosion in an

38

upstairs drinking den in Brighton. It wasn't very serious but that was very much me working outside the realistic mode, and interested in doing so.

You can see that tendency at work in my realistic plays too. Even in *The Party*, because there's something about a speech that lasts for twenty minutes uninterrupted in a so-called natural setting, like a living room, that changes the nature of what's happening. And clearly Gethin Price in the second act of *Comedians*. So I've been interested in challenging realism from within.

It's been my traditional position, however, and I think it's one that I still hold, that when you're trying to speak to large numbers of people who did not study literature at university, because they were getting on with productive work, and you're introducing fairly unfamiliar, dense and complex arguments into the fabric of the play, it's just an overwhelming imposition to present those arguments in unfamiliar forms. That has been my position for the last ten years and in a modified way it remains it. Which doesn't mean that I'm not deeply interested in what is available in new techniques of studio production. Though having seen some of the product I don't feel that I'm missing too much at the moment.

How do you understand the characterization of your work with that rather tricky critical term, 'realist'?

Well I think my practice as realist is probably Lukacsian. I'm not sure I want to say too much about it, but it's that whole idea of a character working as a confluence of important social and political and moral forces within society, in real historical time. That, I suppose, for me, is as persuasive as anything in critical theory. I didn't read Lukacs and say 'Oh I want to write that way.' But reading Lukacs offers some insight into the way one works.

It's really where fiction and history not just intersect but actually converge—I think that is a dramatic text. So you don't invent the history in order to foist the character, and in a sense the character has to come out of the history.

And the danger is that both writer and reader become more interested in the character than in the history?

That's one danger. The other danger is schematism, that a character becomes a device, a vehicle for showing social forces. But since my notion of character is not nineteenth century, that's to say my

39

interest in character is not basically psychological but social, socio-logical and political, I have to find ways both of allowing identifications and establishing critical distances from character in action. That's the way my realisms work, but I seem to be the only person who knows it. Nobody bothers with that: if it's realism, it's realism, and if it's not, it's not—the categories are quite empty in the mouths of most people who use them. To compare my realism with, say, Hugh Whitemore's, is to miss the point, is not to see the import-ant differences.

Finally, you've said that the primary importance of working in a form like television is significantly reaching a large number of people. In a lot of ways Bill Brand *was your most significant attempt to do that. Do you regard it as a success?*

I'm glad that I did it. But I don't think of things in terms of success or failure. You see the most perfect play I've written is *Apricots*, which at the last count has been seen by about seventeen people. So what? A quite good play which is a terrific failure is *Such Impossibil-ities*, because it never got shown. Getting it shown is success in that sense, getting an audience is terrific. Sensing just murmurs and whispers after, that it lives, that it has some purchase still on people's minds, imaginations and possibly even practices, that's terrific. But for every story that you hear of a positive effect, you hear another one which is negative, where entirely the counter-produced meaning has been taken of the play and its characters—that happens quite a bit. That's what plays are, they're very organic, and especially in television. Because there's no training, no training in reception, in response. It's just a massive aggregation of people all sitting down together but remote from each other, all at the same time and in virtually the same space and staying or not staying with the piece and then talking about it afterwards, or thinking about it, and taking it on in their own lives.

Ah! Mischief:
The Role of Public Broadcasting

DAVID HARE

For some years I didn't try to write for television. I had two main objections. First, I thought the studio process was harmful to good work and, second, I didn't like the censorship. I had started writing for the stage long after the Lord Chamberlain had been discredited, so it never occurred to me that a writer should be anything but free. I admire writers in Africa, say, or in Russia or South America who have to accept the limitations of dictatorship and who learn to work guilefully within them, but in a democracy I take the principle of free expression very seriously, even to the point where I doubt the wisdom of the race laws. So I am unlikely to take orders from bureaucrats about what I may or may not say in my plays, especially when as a viewer I am aware of how badly television has deteriorated in the last ten years. The row over *Yesterday's Men*, the banning of *Scum* and the cancellation of E. P. Thompson's Dimbleby lecture are only the most conspicuous of a series of incidents which encourage the feeling that the BBC is run by men who have made an unspoken accommodation with government: in return for securing the necessary annual increase in their licence fee, they have run down the service, and in particular its majority television channel, to the point of maximum inoffensiveness.

When Ian McEwan's play *Solid Geometry* was banned by the BBC in 1979, just two days before it was due to go into the studio, the Head of Network Production Centre, Pebble Mill, made a graphic defence of his decision to me by saying, 'How do you think it would look if just as Margaret Thatcher was about to be elected, we were stupid enough to record a play which featured a twelve-inch penis in a fucking bottle?' (In fact, the script says *less* than twelve inches; but it had lengthened in the mind in the Head of Network Production Centre.) I admired his forthrightness, or rather I admired it until I received a memorandum the next day—I still have it—which reminded me that should this confession of motive be leaked to the press, I would be sacked. Well, time has gone by, I am no longer under contract, and worse and sillier decisions have since been made; but both the memorandum and the blatancy of the conversation confirmed what I had already sensed in the mishandling of the row about *Scum*—that BBC censorship in the late 1970s had passed into a particularly ugly phase.

In 1975, *Brassneck* had been the first of my stage plays to be adapted for television, for an earlier attempt to adapt *The Great Exhibition* had foundered when it was explained to me that references to exhibitionism were permitted in Light Entertainment but not in Drama. *Brassneck* was accepted; the script was in production and, so far as we could see, going well, when the Head of Drama suddenly threatened cuts. A meeting with him was quickly arranged in the Windmill pub on Clapham Common, and he offered to trade. 'I'll swap you two buggers for a shit' is the line I best remember. In fact, we'd cleared up the scatology in five minutes, and the wrangling only really started when we got to the 'God's and 'Oh Christ's. Even then, implicit in this public-house negotiation was the shared understanding that the whole damn business was too silly for words, that censorship was something degrading which we all had to put up with but which we all despised, but that for now we would drag through this meaningless game if for no other reason than to keep the Head of Drama in his job; which we did, and once the bartering was done, we drank more and honoured the agreement.

I cannot imagine such a session taking place any longer in the BBC. A new self-righteous tone has been adopted by men who often seem to take a chilling pleasure in the exercise of their own power. 'Nobody here likes halting a play,' they say, rolling the sentence round in their mouths, enjoying the taste. They appear actually to believe in something they call responsibility, which by the time it reaches our screens we may take to mean blandness, and in something else called editorial control, which I construe as them knowing better than you do, something which an artist (I know no other word to use) finds hard to accept in a journalist.

Differences in temperament between playwrights and journalists have been at the heart of many of the problems there have recently been in TV drama. The BBC is run almost exclusively by ex-journalists—sports men predominate and arts men rarely rise to the top—and there is a sense in which journalists neither understand nor accept the claims of fiction. They are bewildered and hurt by the idea that a playwright offers something which is necessarily partial, which is only an aspect of the truth, because for them, of course, the truth is verifiable. It is a piece of paper which passes across the news desk. They are most unsettled by the storyteller's central claim—that by compressing events and telling unrepresentative stories in personal ways he may reveal truths which are at least as important as the journalist's. The BBC's institutional panic in the face of *Scum*, during what was the most frightening and acrimonious of all its censorship rows, stemmed absurdly from the fact that its executives did not finally understand what a play was, and tried to apply to drama criteria which could only make sense, if at all, when applied to documentaries. Although they conceded that all the events in *Scum* were plausible, that everything in the script had indeed happened and could well happen again, their objections to its transmission were based on the idea that it was somehow wrong to cram all these incidents into one hour's television and thereby suggest they were typical of the whole English Borstal system. But, in fact, plays make no claims to be typical in that sense. The play *Macbeth* is not intended as an indictment of Scottish monarchy, nor does Shakespeare set out to prove that all Scottish kings tend towards murder. Yet an imaginary BBC of the seventeenth century, faced with that script, would have objected that Scottish kings *do not kill each other all that frequently*, and so the play must be banned. There is, they would say disingenuously, no 'balancing voice'. But where is the balancing voice in Dante? In Bunyan? In Dostoevsky?

What is equally sad is how outdated the managerial tone of journalism has become. Because he has been brought up and worked all his life in authoritarian organizations, in the backwoods of Fleet Street, the ex-journalist cannot understand the violence of feeling his bans cause among the storytellers. Alisdair Milne's astonishing insensitivity to his staff during the *Scum* row sprang—I am guessing here—not from any defect of character, but from the fact he had worked primarily among journalists who are well used to the idea that work can be spiked. Journalists have always been told that they must put up with having their work changed, for on a newspaper it is something which happens all the time. But in a theatre it never now happens, except by consent. Indeed, to an outsider, one of the main reasons for the general weakness of the British press appears to be the readiness

43

of journalists to conspire to the massacre of their own work. They accept that their pieces will be cut and altered. They allow contradictory rubbish to be placed alongside their articles in flatulent editorial columns, and when asked why, will tell you it is because they cannot be bothered to get involved in the day-to-day running of their newspaper. Playwrights, by contrast, spend a good deal of their time defending and explaining their plays to management. They see it as part of their job not just to see their work through to the point of presentation, but also to argue about the overall direction of theatres where their work goes on. They expect access to the boss, and they expect to be able to criticize the general policies of the theatre. Senior executives at the BBC are rumoured to hide from their own employees.

These problems in the drama department are now part of a wider unease at the BBC, which has come about through the growing rift between the programme makers and the bureaucracy. In spite of the Annan Committee's harsh views on this subject, it is hard to see any improvement under the present regime. For whatever the statistics (is it one in seven employees at the BBC who is actually involved in programme making?), the major problem is to do not with numbers but morale. Programme makers no longer feel that the bureaucracy sees its job as to serve them. Instead they feel that they themselves have been made the servants of a corporation which seems to be organized chiefly for the convenience of its own executive, and whose incidental product happens by chance to be television programmes. As a film maker, when I receive any message from above, my immediate reaction is that I must be in trouble, for I can imagine no other reason why they are trying to contact me. If I hear one of the great panjandrums wants to talk to me, I assume automatically that his purpose will be to unveil a fresh scheme for butchering my work. I distrust these men, in short, because I do not believe they have my interests at heart. All around me there is evidence that as in all overinflated institutions the chief loyalty of those in charge has come to be to the institution itself and not to its original purpose. The evidence exists that the executive has become deferential to government. They imagine that by placating politicians they will ensure the survival of public broadcasting. They are wrong. And if ever they were once right, the price has been too high to pay.

Television ceases to be of any democratic value if it cannot be trusted. The audience must believe it is watching something which has not been tampered with. The audience at present know full well that a good part of what is reaching them is doctored pap. The pro-censorship lobby always likes to claim that TV is a dangerously powerful medium, which an innocent audience receives uncritically. In the early days this may well have been true, but now the audience, far from being supine, is cagey, highly critical and selective, and often caustic in its attitude to what is shown. Television, like the monarchy, now exists as much to be mocked as to be worshipped. Far from having too much authority, it seems now to have almost no authority at all. Many celebrities who imagined they enjoyed public adulation on television have found out how close the adulation is to contempt. Muggeridge's elaborate disenchantment with the medium in fact seems nothing more than the performer's realization that the nation has perceived him to be a vain fool. There is of course some-thing intrinsically demeaning in striving too blatantly for national approval, but worse, the medium itself is now widely held suspect. The cries of writers whose work has been banned have only added to the public's suspicion of the BBC's integrity. The chronic failures of nerve, as over *Scum*, may dispassionately be put down to a misunder-standing of the nature of fiction, which by definition cannot aspire to the facile ideas of 'balance' so loved by the controllers, but to the public they inevitably appear as something more sinister—as the des-perate bunglings of a frightened organization. The only way the BBC could now retrieve its earlier credibility would first of all be by as-serting its independence from government (banning programmes the Home Office dislikes hardly seems the best way to go about this), and secondly by returning power in the organization from the carpeted sixth floor back to where it rightly belongs: with the programme makers.

For years, the needs and interests of those who create the work at the BBC have been subordinate to the determination of the executive to shape the organization into an industrial machine, and nowhere has this pressure been more disastrous than in the run-down of the film units and the insane over-investment in videotape studios. Years ago the decision was taken to build these stale over-lit shells in a great circle round the ground floor of TV Centre, and industrial logic now demands that they are used to the maximum and that all programmes however dissimilar be jammed into them. Whence *Sportsnight* is broadcast, there too must Play for Today be made. And yet this decision was made in defiance of the artistic preferences of nearly

45

every drama director in the building. For although the public often claims it cannot tell the difference between taped plays and filmed plays, nevertheless when asked to name the single plays they have most enjoyed, nearly all will be films. Annually awards in drama go only to film makers, simply because they have started with the incomparable advantages of working on location, setting up shot by shot, rehearsing as they go, and working for eight weeks at the end to edit their ideas into sequence.

My original feeling that standards were so low that it was not worth working in television at all were based on my early experience of videotape. The play is cast, rehearsed in a couple of weeks, then slung on through a three-day scramble in the studio which is so technically complicated and so artistically misconceived that excellence is rarely achieved except by accident. The eye is always on the clock. The pressure of time and the cost of over-running are so great that a director justifiably feels he has done well if he has got the play made at all. 'Good' directors in the studio are therefore, as far as the management are concerned, those who get their shows in on time. The process of manoeuvring camera and cast along this assault course requires such skill and patience that a rush of adrenalin hits every director at the end of his three days. Should he succeed in cramming the lot in, he leaves the box a giant, ablaze with excitement, crying 'We've done it.' Only an hour later in the bar when the rush is dying does he think 'Yes, but *what* have we done?' The truly hard questions can never be answered in the studio, because the part-hard questions are going to occupy nearly all your time. My own last memory of the recording of *Brassneck* was of leaving the box forty minutes after 'time' had been called, with an unrehearsed scene of a hundred extras and four unplotted cameras still going on chaotically downstairs, and the director crying helplessly to a random cameraman, 'Go in, Number Four, anything you can get.'

I apologized earlier for using the word 'artist' for it is a word which has knocked around with bad company and been discredited. Anyone who dares to call himself an artist risks the charge of arrogance, and yet his arrogance seems to me nothing compared with that of those who demand the artist's allegiance without giving him the facilities to do his best work. In the shambles of the marketplace, there does seem to me an important role for the single voice, uncensored, the voice that promises to speak only when it has something to say, and which insists that when it speaks the conditions in which it is heard are under control. This should not be too much to ask. If the voice matters, if the voice really is wanted, then the organization will accommodate itself. And if this is in defiance of the ratings, if it is a voice less popular than David Coleman's, then the sacrifice will be made, and with good heart. Both of the directors of my early plays (one of them was Alan Clarke, in many ways the best director in television; the play, which was wiped and no longer exists, was *Man above Men*) were directors of the very first class, and yet they were forced to work under conditions which were simply not adequate to the production of good work. I determined never again to be a victim of the industrial process, and when I wrote *Licking Hitler*, I chose to direct it myself, partly of course to protect it against any institutional pressures, but also because I alone was willing to wait a year until one of the coveted film slots came free at BBC Birmingham. In David Rose I found a producer whose allegiance to the film maker is absolute, and whose distrust of the system, based on a far wider experience, was, if anything, greater than my own.

Film is free. Every artist worth anything in the twentieth century has longed to work in it because it is quick and supple. It has wit. Film passes effortlessly from style to style. By angling, by heightening, by the slightest visual distortion your view of your material may alter in the passage of a single shot. Film is fast. It cuts well. You create your work like a mosaic out of tiny pieces, each one minutely examined as it's prepared, and then slipped into the stream of images you are preparing in your head. I made my first film after eight years' work in the theatre, and I was exhilarated by the contrast between the two forms. The theatre is collaborative. There is no special virtue in the director and writer being one man, for it is in the nature of the event that it must be re-created every night by many people, each of whom must understand the exact reason for each artistic decision. If an actor is asked to move quicker in the theatre, he will at once ask why. He will need to have a good reason in his head in order to be able to justify his speed every night. And if the reason is not good, his performance will deteriorate. But on film he will obey without asking, for he knows the basic truth of film making, that only the director can see. Only the director knows how the images are to be composed, more important, only he knows how they are to fit together, and because every image must finally pass through this single brain, the actor accepts that his job is to serve, on trust.

Videotape lies in between theatre and film, the hopeless hybrid, recorded in slabs with unwieldy machinery which, up till now, has lacked visual finesse, against sets which have no stylistic density or texture, and lit from a grid which is too high and too crude. I waited a year, and would have waited five to avoid putting *Licking Hitler* through the studio, although it was often pointed out to me that it was set almost entirely indoors. 'Please go outside', an exasperated controller said to me, 'just for a few shots', as if that would somehow justify the use of film. But a sense of pace in film comes not from fast cars and busy streets, but from the movement of ideas. A film well cut indoors seems faster than a silly action thriller. Videotape, with inferior editing techniques, lumbers. Whatever the plans—and to the BBC's credit they exist—for trying to shoot studio plays in less rigid ways, whatever improvements you make by altering the grids, by changing the cameras, by extending the schedules, by shooting 'four-walls', in the last analysis the highest compliment you will ever be able to pay a studio play is *that it almost looked like film*. Not a true form in itself, it can only aspire to imitate another. Like needlework, studio is painstaking but dull.

The finest TV programme I have seen in years was Robert Vas's posthumous documentary about the work of the National Film Archive. Ironically it was television itself which delivered this fabulous compilation of around 150 clips from some of the films which are stored away in the vaults in Hertfordshire. For the first time, watching the extraordinary wealth of an art form which is only eighty years old, I began to understand the humanist claim that in its overpowering richness film approximates to life itself. Given the collapse of the feature-film industry and the shortcomings of the British distribution system, the BBC is now charged with protecting that tradition. Its job must be to guarantee the skills of the film industry in order that films may go on being made. I can imagine no more honourable or enjoyable task for a public broadcasting organization. Public television should be quite different in its priorities from the commercial sector. Even if it is forced to compete for audiences, its reasonings should be unalike. Ironically it is those who most believed in public broadcasting who were driven away in the late seventies by the threats management made to the freedom of the drama department's work, and it is those same directors and writers who long to return to the BBC.

At the best of times, television will always be a dangerous medium for a writer because he is so isolated from his audience. Any night in the theatre you may gauge moment by moment what the audience thinks of your work, you may watch them slip away in the space of a few minutes, you may *feel* their exasperation or contentment, but the television writer depends on the delayed response of a few selected people, mostly his peers, sometimes his neighbours and usually his friends. He does not know at first hand where the audience has come towards him, and where they have drifted away, he has not had to endure their scrutiny, so he easily deceives himself. He is never put to the test of sharing his impression of the play with six hundred other people. The crazy statistics—eight million viewers for a single play— go to his head, and simultaneously he experiences a sense of unreality. Who are these eight million and what are they thinking? He easily comes to believe that everything on television is passing by in one nightmare stream of which his play is only a tiny part. When Dennis Potter argues that the audience cannot always distinguish between the plays and the dogfood commercials, what he is really doing is projecting his own isolation and bewilderment on to his audience. He assumes that because for him the experience of having a play on television is brutally casual—compared with the sustained excitement of a stage play—so it must be for the audience. And newspapers flatter this view of television by appointing gag-men to be TV critics. The fashion is for writers—some of them brilliant, some of them not—whose underlying assumption is that there is one long spectacle passing by, which, it is supposed, will have variety but not density. The purpose of the stream will be for the critic to make jokes which will keep the stream in its place, where it belongs, in the corner of the room, a toy. So the playwright needs the steadiest of nerves, and a clear head to try and find out just what his audience's true response is. The letters I receive are compelling but eccentric. 'I saw your play and left my job', said one correspondent. Another '. . . saw your play and have left my husband.'

This strange botched-up medium is too good for a writer to resist, but too unreal for him to risk giving his entire loyalty to. Its very confusion is its appeal. Reith, for all his turgid moralism, was nearer to understanding what its priorities should be than the men who now seek to control its tone. Researching *Licking Hitler*, I found that one of the people who knew most about wartime broadcasting was the former Director-General Hugh Carleton-Greene, so nervously I went round to his flat to explain that I was planning a play about black propaganda in the Second World War. 'There can only', he said ominously, 'be one reason why a writer like you could possibly be interested in that subject; to make mischief.' At once he broke into the broadest smile, and rubbed his hands together. I have never seen a man so delighted by a single word. How attractive that spirit is in him, how fine the BBC was when he ran it, how much that sound working principle—'ah, mischief!'—is needed there today.

Television:
An Outsider's View

JULIAN MITCHELL

The history of all institutions is the same. They begin in hope and high purpose, open to outsiders, zealous for the general good. After a year or two, it is announced with deep regret by the now permanent staff of the central policy administration unit that in future more formal procedures will, alas, have to be implemented in the interests of more efficient functioning. After a decade, all openness is over, high purpose is confined to inter-departmental intrigue and personal advancement, and hope has been strangled in a broom cupboard. Though regular obeisance is made to the institution's original purpose, it has come to exist solely for its own benefit. Lifeless immobilism has set in, for life.

Thus, in television, the making of programmes has become a secondary activity. Like the MCC, television exists for members to drink too much before lunch and lounge in front of the pavilion, while the players get on with the game, and the public watches at a respectful distance. For a writer, the bar at Television Centre has a nightmare fascination. All those important people drinking gin after gin, then rolling back down the interminable corridors to mutilate his script! Standing there, safe in their jobs, their pension schemes pressed against their hearts, eating sausages on sticks and controlling his destiny! What do they care about plays, with their lovely leggy secretaries, their big desks, their mysterious wall-charts, their places in the car park? They've got it made, and it's not programmes.

Paranoia, the lethal occupational disease of freelance life, descends in dizzying black clouds. He doesn't belong here! And yet he does. This isn't what it's all about! But it is, it is. Stumbling to get out alive and sane, he finds himself in those damned circular corridors again. On a wall there's a large glass case, full of silver trophies. Hurrying past, he catches a glimpse of the hideous dolphin, symbolizing the triumph of imagination, which *he* was awarded for *his* play at the Bosnian Television Festival of 1977. There it gleams, locked away from his thieving inky hands by the proud institution which considers *it* won it. Stumbling on past door after smug office door, with names and numbers and a sense of belonging, he can't find the lavatory, let alone the way out. And in his panic and fear, a terrible truth bursts with unbearable brightness through the black swirl; there *is* no way out. If he wants to be in television at all, he has to accept the institution's terms and conditions of service as well as its cash. The only serious question is, are they worth it?

When I first went into television I was less jaundiced. It was the end of the sixties and I had a small reputation as a novelist. My six novels had been fairly well reviewed, but they'd been read, at a generous estimate, by 0.25 per cent of the population. They earned me just about enough to keep me in ribbons and carbon. (Photocopying was quite beyond a respectable novelist's means and therefore not nice.) I made my living on the fringe of literature—reviewing, broadcasting, bits of teaching and lecturing. Now and then I spent a terrible month or two trying to write impossible films for implausible producers, not all of whom paid up. My great stroke of luck had been being asked to adapt Ivy Compton-Burnett for the stage. I had always wanted to write plays—I'd been trying since my teens. But of the two adaptations the first was not a financial success and the second failed even to reach the West End. Though I'd spent a summer in Greece on a Maugham Award, the play I wrote there was no good. An autumn at the court of Franco Zeffirelli had left me much wiser about the world, but with no script and nothing more than expenses. I was depressed. I didn't want to spend the rest of my life writing one sort of thing for money so I could afford to write another for myself. The prospect of shelves of other people's books stretching out to eternity, demanding to be reviewed, quite put me off reading altogether. The literary world was, in any case, insufferably narrow and bitchy, and the English novel, if not actually dying, fading quietly away. One read bulletins on its passing in every magazine. Only half-way to the grave, I felt at a premature dead end.

Television offered a wonderful escape. Patronizing about it at first, regarding it as just another literary fringe and myself as a serious novelist on holiday, I rapidly became more respectful. The serious novel is a cottage industry. The writer weaves away, responsible only to himself for his warp and woof. In England, unless he's a best-seller, and not always then, his publisher will scarcely ever ask him to change so much as a comma in his manuscript. The novelist is an Artist, and the publisher's duty is simply to decide whether or not the Artwork takes his fancy and will adorn his list. No one expects to make money. If, by accident, a serious novel does make money, it's rather frowned on. The author's next book will be received with stern reviews, there will be mutterings about disappointed expectations. The novelist, like the fringe playwright, should be a lone heroic figure, battling against public misunderstanding. If understanding comes, there must be something wrong with the novel or play.

On the whole the novelist doesn't drive because he can't afford to. The film writer, of course, drives a Thunderbird. He has given his soul for it. In the movie business 'Art' is confined to use as a forename, and the writer doesn't write, he produces a script by a certain date. A script is only provisional, never finished. It is the basis for what may or may not happen in a studio or on a location. More likely, it will pass through someone else's typewriter, emerging unrecognizable the other end. It is never the writer's, like a novel. Whatever the credits may say, a script is a collaboration in which the writer or writers are very junior to the director and producer. (The one film which went out with my name attached contained no line of my original dialogue, and had the assistance of at least six other writers besides my first collaborator and me. There was a single producer-director.) You can be very expensive as a movie writer—I never was, alas—but you are always expendable. You are also made to feel your place; many producers go out of their way to humiliate you. Only huge sums of money floating on vast swimming-pools can begin to console you for the abuse of your talent, if you ever had any.

I exaggerate, of course—minutely. There are examples of mutually respectful, equal collaboration between writer and director; mainly when these are one and the same person. But the writer always knows that the director has the final word (if not always the final cut). The word is subservient to the picture, and frequently to the music. Where a novel's shape is what the writer intended (or as near as he can get it), a filmscript is merely the launchpad for another man's talent (if *he* has any). And for all that there are better screenwriters and worse ones, for all that there is a real craft involved, nothing will ever change that, except the writer directing his own picture.

Television turned out to be far more than a half-way house between these extremes. It didn't just offer a huge audience and a reasonable living, it added respect for one as a writer. Out of the ghetto of the novel, out of the luxurious prison of the film, on to the airwaves! Or was it into them? No matter, millions of people were watching! It's true you couldn't see or hear them, but they were there, the figures proved it. And if they were gawping rather than watching, who but Marxist academics, busy shouldering their way forward, would be cruel enough to say so? (Haven't *they* done well!!) 'If only the buggers would send an occasional postcard,' said another television writer one day. We were passing through London, was it? Leicester? Liverpool? Television aerials spread as far as the eye could see. Our programmes were going down those very chimneys, night after night, and we never got so much as a puff of smoke in response. But if the public accepted my work passively, perhaps even with resignation, the institution liked it. I was suddenly in demand—something that had never happened to me in my life before. Instead of sitting undisturbed for months, wondering whether it was all worthwhile, whether anyone, anywhere, would ever even notice, there was suddenly someone ringing up, knocking on the door, looking over my shoulder and saying 'I don't think this scene works, have another go at it.' I had to defend my writing line by line—not from a sniffy reviewer with 200 words, months after I'd finished writing, but to people whose job it was to make it better *now*, before the world saw it, people whose own reputations were involved as well as mine. We were making the play together—just like in the theatre. I liked that very much, just as I liked the economy of writing dialogue instead of narrative prose. I even came to like rewriting. I began to look with a certain detachment at my own first drafts, to see them as cold iron, rough horseshoes to be hammered into shape.

Of course there were times when I thought the first draft was as good as the play was ever going to be. Of course some script-editors and producers and directors are crass and ignoble. Of course I sometimes longed to be the sole arbiter of my own work again. But in any collaboration—and the number of collaborators in television is as large as in film, if not larger—you have to surrender absolute autonomy. Isolation and loneliness, though, are surrendered, too. If you've been on your own for years, to be part of a team, and generally acknowledged the most vital part, is a profound pleasure. And you are so acknowledged, because television is the opposite of film; the word is supreme over the picture, and the vast majority of TV directors aim to serve the script not themselves. There are exceptions, of course; particularly among those who've made their living in advertising and are on their way to Hollywood. (But some of the best directors have started in advertising, too.)

As a result of all this close reading and rewriting, most television scripts are far better written, far better constructed, than most novels. It is just that much harder to get away with self-indulgence, flabby prose, padding, inconsistency, implausibility. Naturally, television drama departments can't create good writing, only better writing, and most remains, as it always has in novel and theatre, bad.

My confidence, which had been low, perked up at all the attention I was getting, and a very good thing too. Confidence in your own work is absolutely essential in television as in the theatre. You have to be confident to be flexible, and you have to be confident to be firm. When I began, some directors tried to keep me away from rehearsals, and in my ignorance I did go away, and had no one but myself to blame when things went wrong which I could have prevented. The writer has every right and reason to be present during all stages of the making of his play. How much time he actually spends on it will depend on the trust he has established with his director and producer. Some people deliver the script, attend discussions, do their rewrites, then go home and start on something else. They hand over completely; no doubt it's an excellent way to increase one's productivity. But I enjoy the whole process of making a play. I like watching actors and actresses at work, I like to check the details of the sets— I've lent my own pictures on occasion. I even enjoy the tension and frustration of the studio. (Television films—made on location, not in the studio—are different. The process of filming is unbearably slow and boring for all but a handful of those involved, and the writer has little to contribute. Which isn't to say that phone-calls for new lines or alterations aren't always a welcome excuse for an excursion to the location.)

Trust between writer and director is very much helped by the fact that they are both freelances, struggling together against the inertia of the institution. Rows between them are happily rare. (I've only once wanted to take my name off a play, and that was not the director's fault.) Relations with a producer can be more problematical. A producer may be part of the institution, an employee to be treated with caution; in that case you hope he's a good bureaucratic politician, for much of the success of any play depends on the producer's ability to get the institution to cough up the requisite money and facilities. Sometimes, though, the producer will be a freelance himself, in which case he will be engaged in a constant battle with the permanent staff of the institution who will try to frustrate him at every turn. The permanent staff detest all outsiders. They give them the worst office space, furthest from the canteen. They allot them the oldest equipment and the most incompetent technicians. Once the producer has finally got what he wants, it's immediately taken away again. Like all great bureaucracies, television has less and less will to do anything positive itself, more and more to prevent anyone else doing it. It's no accident that many of the best independent producers are women; men can't stand that amount of frustration, they're not used to it.

Even when a writer has doubts about his producer and director, he has one great thing on his side. The television screen is small. The picture doesn't overwhelm the audience, as in the cinema; the sound doesn't come washing round the living-room in luscious stereophonic waves. (The sound on most television sets is disgracefully poor, as a matter of fact.) People *listen* to television. It's much more like radio with pictures than it is like movies. In modern movies, the words are often deliberately inaudible; the director wants to tell his story with pictures and sound, not pictures and dialogue. He is interested in large-scale dramatic effects, in impressions, not in the sharp particularity of dialogue. But in TV, large-scale effects simply don't work; the screen won't take them. What the screen *will* take is people talking comprehensibly to each other.

This means that films for television have to be gauged at the same level as studio plays. And that brings me to one of the most frustrating aspects of all television drama. Making plays in the studio is a maddening business. There's always a boom-shadow over the heroine's face on her best take, for instance, because no one has yet been able to think up a better way of recording sound than to stick microphones on long booms and waggle them over the actors' faces at the crucial moment. (The person who *does* think up something better will be an instant millionaire.) More serious, and to writer, director and actors far more frustrating, is the loss of quality in performance between rehearsal room and studio. Studios are extremely expensive to run, and the institution requires as many programmes to be made in them as possible. As a result, there is never enough time given to the programme makers to make their programmes. (I can scarcely remember a recording in which we didn't overrun for one reason or another.) The cast never have enough time to rehearse with the cameras, the cameras never have enough time to rehearse with the cast.

In rehearsal rooms, actors and director are able to concentrate on their work, bringing it to a fine pitch for the producer's run on the final day. Without costumes, without props, using any old chairs and tables, this final run is often extremely dramatic and moving—just what everyone wants. We all go away thinking the play is going to be wonderful. Next day we're in the studio. Machines trundle about, glaring at the actors. It's extremely hot under the lights. The director's camera-plan is painstakingly rehearsed. The play, which has been a coherent entity in that final run, falls apart into its constituent scenes. Finally we begin to record, just as tempers are beginning to fray. At once there's a hair in the gate or a fly in the lens or, inevitably, a strike. There's always a strike, because television is an institution with institutionalized labour relations and institutionalized attitudes. Not to have a strike would be a dangerous breach of precedent; neither management nor unions would tolerate that. Even supposing there isn't a strike, the atmosphere in the studio is always bad. There is deep resentment of all these dreadful, unreliable, non-institution people—actors and actresses. And they've lost their main support. The director, who's nursed them through rehearsals, has vanished. He's miles away, it feels like miles, high up in the control room. He doesn't even speak to his cast direct, but through a man with headphones. What yesterday was living and breathing, close and palpable, is suddenly a humming bank of electronic images. The technical has got ponderously in the way of the human.

And all the time the institution is watching—some remote executive is turning a knob and peering, unseen, at what's going on. More sinister, the studio is full of people who seem to have nothing to do but look at the cast with hostility.

All freelances tend to anarchism, left-wing or right-wing according to taste. We are driven to it by the ruthless statism of the organizations for which we work. We don't really belong anywhere. The tax authorities loathe us for not being convenient and on PAYE. The social security system is designed to exclude us as far as possible. And it's entirely our own fault. We have done those things we ought not to have done. We have disregarded all sensible advice, we have flown in the face of our parents' fears for our own wellbeing. We have not taken steady jobs with pension schemes. We have not got something to fall back on. We have committed ourselves to lives of stupid, and in some eyes anti-social, economic risk. We can't complain about it, though we do, ceaselessly, because it's what we've chosen—a life of doing what we want rather than what someone else wants for us. And the eyes round the studio condemn us.

Our only real justification is that we put our work before ourselves. When we do something, we want it to be as good as it possibly can be. We don't see the point of doing it otherwise. Also, if people see our work as we want it to be seen, they will, we fondly believe, see that it *is* good. They will want to see more. We will be in demand. Artistic and commercial motives are thus united.

But most of the people staring at us have no artistic motive at all. And their commercial motive has been removed by the institutionalization of their jobs. Some of them actually *don't* have anything to do—their jobs don't exist. They're there because they're there because union and management have agreed that that's where they shall be, though they have nothing to do but be bored all day and contribute their union dues. They are a minority—I hope. But they do contribute something: intense demoralization. The majority are only slightly less demoralized themselves. They are only required for short bursts of activity between long waits. Well paid though they are for their inactivity, they are terribly, terribly bored. And they see us, tense, excited, involved, and they hate us because we're passionate and they're not, we're freer than they are. Their boredom is institutionalized. It's part of an agreement drawn up years ago between cynical management and cynical unions in a foolish attempt to avoid strikes which ought to have taken place. The air is now so thick with cynicism, corruption and mistrust it will never be cleared. It is recycled, stale, institutional air.

Of course those with something to do are not (you sincerely hope) bored and demoralized. As a matter of fact, one of the pleasures of being in a studio is watching technicians practising their various crafts; a cameraman testing his skill on an empty set, for instance, pulling his focus from here to there, trying new angles, enjoying himself. But for the majority of the institution's work-force, one day's work is the same as any other. There is nothing special about the occasion, unless, perhaps, there's a nude scene. Otherwise—the job's a job, and that's all there is to it. Though let one of the freelances dare to move a bunch of flowers on the set, and see what institutional wrath comes thundering forth! Before you know where you are you've got another strike on your hands, or at least a meeting to decide whether or not to strike. The one thing the work-force has to look forward to is its breaks. At last something to do—eating and drinking! That's why the confrontation often becomes most open and vicious at lunchtime. Hours of work are, naturally, institutionalized. But if you're nearing the end of a scene, if you want to finish something before the break, the producer can ask the union representatives to postpone it for five or ten minutes. There will always be very good technical or artistic reasons for the request—no one would dare make it otherwise—but the number of times it will be refused would astonish anyone outside the industry. The making of programmes is completely secondary. Adherence to the rule-book comes first. To the freelance, who is himself, of course, a union member, such clock-watching is simply incomprehensible. 'What are we here for?' he cries, beating his head against the glass panels of the control-room. As much as we can get, says the work-force, going. Life, says the institution.

The truth is, bad labour relations are enjoyed by both sides of television. The management likes to confront, the work-force likes to be suspicious; it makes both of them feel alive and important. The freelance doesn't care whose the intransigence is, he just wishes it would stop. But it won't. The workings of the institution are of far greater concern to the institutionalized than its purpose. No one is interested in bridging the gap between rehearsal room and studio, between what a piece could be and what it will be. The difference is generally reckoned at about 20 per cent. The public, that is, is getting about 80 per cent of what it should be getting. And if the public doesn't know, and the institution is indifferent—what can the writer possibly do?

He can go into television films. And that, as the seventies went on, is what writers, directors and producers increasingly did. On location, away from the intimidation of the physical fact of the institution, some of the institutional problems fall away. Strikes still occur, of course—they're mandatory. Corruption is more open, too—the fiddling of expenses, the doctoring of bills. But one comes to prefer that to the lowering sullenness of the studio. It's much easier to achieve some sense of common purpose on location. And technically and artistically the results are far, far better. Instead of trying to shoot a whole scene at once, when a hundred different things can go wrong, you shoot it shot by shot till you've got it right. Though the process is slow and expensive, the results are worth it—you get 99 per cent instead of 80 per cent. Then there's the editing—an extremely enjoyable process which needn't, in theory, ever end. (You can go on arranging bits of film together in different orders for years and years.) More important, if something has gone wrong during shooting, you can disguise it. You can markedly improve a performance; you can even improve your structure by reordering scenes. Film has another advantage, too. When you've finished, when you've edited and dubbed and put on the music, you have the very great pleasure of seeing your work on a big screen before it goes out. You sit in a comfortable chair in a small viewing theatre, seeing it under ideal conditions.

The trouble is, that is not how the public sees it, which is a great frustration. Television film *needs* a larger screen than an ordinary TV set. All the beauty of design, all the art of the director and cameraman and costume designer cry out for it. What they get is ordinary sets in ordinary living-rooms; Japanese portables with tiny black and white pictures; radio with a grey flicker. The love and care and art and imagination are still there, but dreadfully diminished. And though the writer suffers least from the process, even he wonders why everyone bothered when so much was lost. The obvious thing, of course, would be to show such films in cinemas as well as on TV, but the institutionalization of labour relations has so far made that unacceptable. As a result, a lot of the very best of recent television has been properly seen by only a handful of people. It could be argued that it wasn't really television at all, but something else. In any case, the frustrations are leading people to think again about the studio, because what's made there is made for television and nowhere else.

But the thought of all the unhappiness staring resentfully at those of us doing what we want is very depressing. Even more depressing is a general demoralization throughout the business, resulting directly from its enormous popular success. Politicians are terrified of television. Those who live by the media shall die by the media, they think, so the best thing is to draw all their teeth. They can't do much about newspapers, but the BBC gets its money from the state, it's an institution within an institution. It can be threatened and blustered at. It can be made to live in fear. And it is.

Television technicians often keep tapes of comic off-screen incidents—people losing their tempers, muffing their lines, fouling things up. I remember listening, for instance, to a celebrated tape of Harold Wilson losing his temper with David Dimbleby. It was a highly revealing occasion, as Wilson himself realized—he threatened dreadful things if it ever got into *Private Eye,* which of course it did. At the time we all laughed loudly; it's always good to catch a public figure with his trousers down. But Wilson and others have had their revenge. Over the last decade politicians of both parties have leaned heavily on television whenever it's looked like getting uppish. Little boys who stick their tongues out—even worse, those who draw attention, however guardedly, to an emperor's fascinating absence of conventional clothing—those little boys get their pocket money docked. In the Council Chamber of the BBC in Broadcasting House, Lord Reith frowns sternly across at Sir Hugh Greene. Under Greene the BBC was more open, more light-hearted, more 'satirical' than it would dare to be now. It's as though Reith, the archetypal institution man, is giving him a dressing down. I told you Whitehall wouldn't like it, he seems to say. And if he did, he was right.

Under the circumstances, there is remarkably little censorship of actual programmes. Considering how craven the Foreign Office is and how many foreign countries there are to take offence; how tireless Mrs Whitehouse has been; how closed our government is and intends to be; well, there are incidents, of course, but—nothing very serious, one might think? The reason is, the censorship starts long before the programmes are made. It is institutional censorship, the 'realism' of institutional men. When in doubt, make another historical series instead. Never cause needless offence. When a writer asks, as innocently as he dare, just what offence is needless and what isn't, he will get the standard institutional reply: 'My dear chap, when one comes down to it, *all* offence is needless, really, isn't it?' Since the BBC sets, and always has set, the tone for television as a whole, and ITV considers that offence very rarely pays, television is very much less lively than it could be.

This censorship is so subtle, so evasive, it's extremely hard to pin down. A few years ago I had what I thought was a brilliant idea for a savagely black comedy about Northern Ireland. I hurried to a producer. A brilliant idea indeed, he said; but alas, to make its point it needed to be made at once, and by an extraordinary chance he had no slot available for at least a year, and amazingly nor had anyone else. The very far-sighted policy of planning all schedules for years ahead, for stock-piling programmes, for not leaving a chink in the armour through which a nasty, directly relevant idea can slip through to the viewers, was proved triumphantly successful. Why not try the radio, he said. So I tried the radio. *What* a brilliant idea, said the producer there, I do like it, I like it very much indeed, but ... we think, on purely artistic grounds, the piece would be much more effective if more universalized. What? If you set it somewhere else. Where? Anywhere except Northern Ireland. But—but—but—Setting it in Northern Ireland makes it so obvious, we feel. But I want to be obvious, the thing's a grotesque cartoon! Sorry, but that's our feeling.

There was no question of censorship, of course. None whatever. But whatever it was was totally effective.

Of course my feeling that television is less lively than it used to be may simply be due to the fact that I'm less lively. But almost everyone I know, inside and outside the business, feels the same—except for one or two very high functionaries within the institution who think it's more wonderful than ever. The public may be getting more critical, please God it is after all these years; whereas it used to be excited just to turn the set on, perhaps it's at last becoming discriminating. What is beyond dispute within the business is that it's much more of an effort to get good programmes made than it used to be, not just because they're expensive (they always were) and there isn't the money around (there never was), but because the inertia of the institution has steadily sapped the energies of the programme makers. When I wrote an episode of *Elizabeth R* in August 1970 I was able to attend rehearsals and recording that November and watch the transmission the following March—the whole process took eight months. Ten years later, *The Good Soldier,* a work I'm equally proud of, took almost four years to get on the screen, what with one thing and another. I have another play which has been waiting to be made for three years and has at least another year to wait before it's even filmed, let alone shown.

This dispiriting lethargy, like the nightmarish labour relations, is peculiarly British. If you write for American TV you're liable to find your producer's been fired before you've finished the script, and the whole project's been dropped; in which case you take the money and fly home first-class at the Americans' expense. But if the play goes ahead, it's on the air within the year. The will to make programmes is there; also the energy. If they commission you to write, they want a play. In Britain you feel all too often that you are being commissioned only out of duty, that plays are a nuisance the institution would rather do without. If only they weren't so popular!

One way of making them less popular, now developed to a high art by the programme schedulers, is to make sure that whenever the BBC puts out a play, ITV puts one out too, thus cutting each audience by half. Freelances have complained about this till they're hoarse, but the institution likes it that way. The institution has been clever with drama producers, too. Once the politicians began to put the squeeze on the BBC, the ITV companies were able to offer much better salaries, and rapidly bought over many of the best producers and technicians. The BBC, which had trained them, could do nothing to defend itself. Nor could the producers do much to defend themselves when they arrived at the other side. Hired, as they thought, to make good programmes, they found what they were actually required to do was make cheap ones. Every obstacle was put in their way, and as soon as there was the slightest drop in the advertising revenues all the interesting, all the imaginative, all the ambitious projects were dropped. The result is—less programmes made by more producers. A series I wrote for an ITV company has now been bought and dropped *three times*; it was even advertised once. The will to talk about it is strong; the will to make it non-existent. The will of the institution is to run a tight ship, a neat and tidy organization in which the serious business of making careers can be pursued with as little distraction as possible from the sordid business of entertaining and informing the public.

If things are really so bad, why do playwrights continue to write for television? After all, there's nothing in the world so exhilarating as a live audience observing and absorbing your play in a theatre. The truth is, as Richard Hughes said many years ago—in his case abandoning drama for novels—'You can earn a fortune in the theatre, but not a living.' Nothing has changed for writers since he said it. Of course, for institutional men there have been wonderful opportunities in recent years. The Arts Council has seen to it that you can make a very cosy living *running* a theatre. And those two great multi-theatrical corporations, the RSC and the National, have demonstrated just how successful dramatic institutions can be. Apart from anything else, they have drained the last remaining energy from the commercial theatre, which has given them an excuse to have fun as well as to put on classics. Unfortunately, neither of them is, at heart, at all interested in new plays. They put on a few as a duty, but whenever cuts are threatened, it's the new work which is first under the axe. At the National, they do at least read unsolicited plays, and return them with courteous, often encouraging letters. At the RSC they don't bother. There, new plays remain unread and unreturned for ever, while the functionaries, heavy with honours and awards, clamour for more subsidy for new venues in which to put on old ones. It's institutional behaviour *par excellence*—censorship by deliberate neglect. Nor is it the only form of censorship in the contemporary theatre. Everyone hoped for a thousand flowers to bloom, once the Lord Chamberlain was gone. But alas, in his place there appeared the new puritans, fierce men and women who believe the world began in Grosvenor Square in 1968. They frown from their offices in half the theatre companies in the country. If you happen not to share their historical perspective, if your plays are insufficiently political—or political in the wrong way—save your stamps, your play will not be done. There's just as much cause for paranoia in the theatre as television, in fact; probably more.

Whoever you write for, there's always something wrong: not enough money, not enough love, not enough attention. The question the writer has to ask himself is, can he work for television without betraying the things for which he became a writer in the first place? In my case the answer is yes. On the whole, I write institutionally acceptable television. I adapt other people's novels, for instance—a highly enjoyable way of practising literary criticism. But it's as a historical playwright that I'm best known, and I don't mind that at all. Having tried and failed to be a real historian, I was snooty about the genre at first. Then I thought of Shakespeare and lay back and enjoyed it. One could wish for a wider range of historical subjects, it's true; kings and queens and lords and ladies and famous politicians and whores make it feel like dramatized A-levels at times. (Of course, *The Merry Mistresses of Charles II* might be fun. Or has it been done already?) But I feel no sense of shame, I hope I am entertaining and informing in these plays.

I don't like faction, that deliberately confusing mixture of fact and fiction which leaves the audience uncertain whether it's seeing a documentary or a play. In television one is always battling for the audience's attention against phone, family, dog, pub, ads, other channels—even, now and then, against books and the theatre. The temptation to *seem* documentary, at a time when it's easy to fake newsreels to look more authentic than the real thing, is very great. But because television is so intensely naturalistic, because fact and fiction follow each other in a ceaseless parade of images, it's extremely important that the audience does *not* confuse the two. There are enough people who think Ena Sharples is real and Violet Carson a fantasy already. Schiller may have made Mary Queen of Scots meet Elizabeth I, but that was in the theatre, where a play about Northern Ireland isn't followed by the latest news from there. Faction is cheating and irresponsible, for the most part. One has to assume that the audience for a historical play knows nothing whatever about the subject in advance, and stick within the known facts. One may inter-pret the characters within those facts as one wishes—imaginative interpretation of the past for the present is exactly what historical plays should be. They should not be lies and fakery. If a playwright feels strongly about some subject he can always write a documentary; there are no demarcation disputes yet in the Writers' Guild, and he has as much duty to truth as to his own imagination.

Though single plays have always attracted the most critical atten-tion, I've never been very happy with them. They're more like short stories than stage plays or novels, and I was never much good at stories. The few I've had made were, with one exception, too quirkily humorous for the general public—upper middle Bohemia is a pro-foundly unpopular subject. I feel the small screen is too small for anything very complex or large to be said within the confines of a single play. But large statements and complexity can be attempted in the television novel, by which I mean something slightly different from the ordinary series. The television novel comes in episodes, like the nineteenth-century novel. It can carry on where it left off last week, or start again somewhere else. It can range about in space and time; it can have a huge cast of characters. It's a large, baggy, flexible, comfortable form in which the writer's imagination can be stretched. Furthermore the public likes it—it has regular characters, a steady individual flavour. Yet it doesn't drag on past all interest and inspi-ration like soap opera or conventional series. Though I've only written one, and that a historical one, I should like to do more. Writers in their maturity (?) should be allowed to settle to major work, instead of being persuaded to go on producing one-off flashes of brilliance. There's another thing: single plays, however good, are soon forgotten. People remember television novels.

If you like writing dialogue, which many novelists don't, then tele-vision can certainly be an honourable way to write. You can still enjoy yourself at it, too, if you're lucky. It may require more effort than it did, but the comradeship is still there, and even if the institution is

65

unfaithful, the audience isn't. (Residuals are wonderful, too.) The truth is, as the world becomes more and more institutionalized, the freelance is more and more on his own. It's an honourable place to be, in television or out of it.

Television Times

PETER PRINCE

Television Times was written partly as an affectionate tribute to the world of TV drama—though as the action included an attempted suicide, a partial blinding and a good deal of teasing of such hallowed institutions as the annual BAFTA Awards ceremony, some people failed to spot the affection. Perhaps I allowed more rancour to creep into the script than I had intended, but I think the two emotions—affection and rancour—are often close together in the hearts of people who have written for television when they contemplate a medium at once so rewarding and so frustrating. Of late, and in public, it has been the rancour that has been most frequently voiced, usually in support of some such important objective as artistic integrity or opposition to censorship and arbitrary banning. I have to report (it may be the company I keep) that while in conversations with fellow-writers I have heard much anger and bitterness expressed about working for TV, it has not been about those matters which are, it seems, thought fit for public consumption. Some of what I *have* heard I put into *Television Times*.

During the studio taping of an episode he's written for *United Kingdom*, a multi-part historical series, the veteran and somewhat jaded TV writer Paul Prior finds himself cooped up in the producer's cubicle with a young aspirant to the craft, Nick Croucher, author of a recently heralded first novel.

PAUL: So you want to get into this lark?
NICK: (*Shyly*) I think so.
    (PAUL *nods.*)
PAUL: Well ... it's a living. (*Pause.*) But not a very good one.
NICK: No?
PAUL: Not with your single plays ... You get your cheque. Looks quite a big one. At first sight. But it's all you'll see.

You might get a repeat. Probably not. You won't get any foreign sales. Your cheque lasts you two, three months. Then you're back where you started.

(PAUL *drags on his cigarette.*)

No, if you want to make money, write for the theatre.

NICK: Yes?

PAUL: Yeah ... I know this bloke. He hasn't written anything for five, six years. He's still doing very well on a couple of stage plays he wrote when he was about nineteen. The money comes in, you know ... Germany, Australia. *Poland* ... Extraordinary.

(NICK *absorbs all this.* PAUL *studies the end of his cigarette sadly. Then glances at* NICK.)

George Crozier? That play of his? Bloke on top of the Post Office Tower ... Should he jump? Shouldn't he jump? He wrote that for Play for Today about five years ago. Got around twelve hundred quid for it. One day his agent gets the idea to send it to a theatre ... Know how much George made on that play last year? ... *One million quid.* It's playing in thirteen countries!

(*Another drag on the cigarette.*)

Plus there's the fame.

(NICK *looks up at him.* PAUL *nods.*)

You could write for this thing ... (*He waves at the TV monitor*) for a hundred years, you wouldn't get a shred of notice ... Couple of lucky nights in some basement, you're set up for life. (*Bitterly.*) I've seen it happen.

(*Looks at* NICK.)

Colin Donnelly?

(NICK *reacts.*)

Big name? Voice of his generation? ... He can't get a thing done here. They've got piles of his scripts upstairs. I've seen 'em. Won't touch him round here ... What does he care? He's packing 'em in in some basement.

(*Pause.*)

NICK: (*Hesitantly*) I have just written a stage play.

PAUL: Yeah? What's it about?

NICK: Oh ... about a bunch of sort of rough kids.

PAUL: Why not?

NICK: They're thinking of doing it here though.

PAUL: Don't you let 'em. You take it to a theatre.

(NICK *nods*. PAUL *adds wistfully*:)

I did a play once about a bunch of rough kids. They put it on BBC-2. 10.30 on a Sunday night. Thank you very much!

(*Pause.*)

And the reviewers! . . . Ever been to a press preview?

(NICK *shakes his head.*)

They come in, full of booze. Usually fall asleep. Go back home in a taxi dead drunk. And then they shit on you from their great height.

(*Pause. Then* PAUL *distinctly*:)

I'm not *bitter* . . . I just wish I'd used my fucking loaf.

Later, after Paul has been chided by his director, Mark Craven, for depressing young Nick, he tries to make amends by showing the lad the other side of the television coin. (Once again, it may seem that Paul's remarks lack profound moral or aesthetic resonances; but it's my observation that—except when addressing the public from a newspaper podium—writers are generally rather shy about revealing the deeper satisfactions they get from their craft.)

PAUL: Look—er . . . I didn't mean to put you off.

(NICK *watches him.*)

About working for here . . . I mean it's good fun on the whole, and—uh . . . there's lots of opportunity. Fourth channel, all that . . . Maybe you *should* let them do that play about kids.

(NICK *still watching.*)

They'll give you a good, solid production. And you'll get name actors. In the theatre . . . very iffy, isn't it?

NICK: I'll have to think about it.

PAUL: Right . . . The thing is: whatever *occasional* complaints one might have, this is the only thing that really counts, isn't it? Born of the age we live in, eh? I mean, what else is there . . . ?

At this point, *United Kingdom*'s producer, Roy Bond, appears in the cubicle to make a phone call to a colleague in Paris—a device that serves not only to interrupt Paul's monologue but also to suggest what I think of as British TV's attractions: its energy, its power and, unusual in this age and country, its widespread international influence.

> (ROY *checks his phone book. Then his watch. Dials fourteen figures. A quick smile at* NICK *as it rings.*)
> (PAUL *is holding up his thumb.*)

PAUL: Books? How many people'll buy your novel? Two thousand? Fifteen hundred? Less?

> (NICK *looks shamefaced.* ROY *puts his hand over his free ear as the phone is answered.*)

ROY: 'Ello. Pouvez-vous me passer l'extension deux-sept-cinq-trois... Merci.

> (PAUL's *forefinger joins his thumb.*)

PAUL: Cinema? Wrong country...

> (PAUL's *next finger goes up.*)

Theatre? Who'll you get? Few Japs. Marxists... They think it's a good night most places if they get a couple of hundred people in.

ROY: Michel! Roy Bond... Oui! Ça va?... Now Michel. I got your telex. And I'm frankly *puzzled.*

> (ROY *listens.* NICK *would like to listen to* ROY. *But* PAUL *is inexorable.*)

PAUL: I had a play on once that was number two in the ratings... (*Honestly.*) Mostly because Clive Heap was in it... *Eighteen million* people watched it. I mean!

ROY: Yes, I appreciate that, Michel, but I thought you understood *my* problem...

PAUL: (*To* NICK) Do you know Clive?

ROY: Filming dates are July, August... I *can't* change them... The *point is*, Michel, they're withdrawing five battalions from NATO manoeuvres as a very special favour and I simply can't just go to them and say...

> (NICK *is distracted between the two conversations.*)

NICK: (*To* PAUL) Sorry?

ROY: I'll be in *very serious trouble.*

PAUL: Clive.

NICK: Er... isn't he Hereward?

PAUL: Yup. And Julius Caesar. Richard the Lionheart. Henry

VIII. Sir Walter Raleigh. And so forth. He plays the main role in every episode. Mark's idea. Bit of a running gag in my opinion... But he *is* a wonderful actor.

(ROY's *face is darkening.*)

ROY: Well, I must say I'm surprised... No, not *angry*. Surprised.

PAUL: Did you see that play I did? Couple of years ago?

NICK: *Fantasies of Power and Vengeance?*

PAUL: (*Pleased*) That's the one.

NICK: I didn't.

ROY: Three and a half million ... pounds.

PAUL: Ah ... well ... well, it was all on film. Clive was so great. In any reasonable country, he'd be a monster movie star. Here ... well, he is very good in those situation comedies. But it's *sad* ...

ROY: Yes ... well, what I think is we should sleep on it ... think it over ... I'll get back to you.

(PAUL *shakes his head. Then smiles.*)

PAUL: We're very close, Clive and me. Very close. In a way I always write for him. You know? With him in mind.

ROY: Tomorrow? ... Peut-être ... How is Denise?

(PAUL *grins shyly.*)

PAUL: *He* says we even look a bit like each other...

(PAUL *revels in the thought.*)

ROY: Excellent... OK, Michel ... Lovely to talk to you... Au revoir... Ciaou... Bye...

(ROY *hangs up. Then stands and stares at the floor. Suddenly:*) Shit! Hell! Fuck!

(*He starts slowly for the door. Glances at* NICK. *An easy smile comes on his face. He half-waves.*) Everything all right?

(NICK *nods quickly.* ROY *exits.* PAUL *reaches for a cigarette.*)

PAUL: No, it's a good life really, TV. You'll enjoy it ... And you get your little treats. We're all off to Italy in a couple of months. Episode 4. Richard the Lionheart. He went on these crusades ... Do a few scenes out there...

(*He lights up. Blows out a long plume of smoke.*) This is your choice. Free trip to Naples. Or a basement in Islington or wherever...

(NICK *ponders this wisdom.*)

And there *is* money in it too. If you're shrewd. *Series*... If you've got the stamina... See, when Roy came with the offer, *United Kingdom*, British history from Year One in fifteen episodes, my initial reaction was—definitely not. *But* I looked into it with my agent... You get your first lot of cheques, fifteen in a row. OK? Then you've got almost certain repeat fees. And practically guaranteed foreign sales, because they soak this costume stuff up... We worked it out...

(*He leans over and taps* NICK's *knee.*)

If you got yourself one of these deals, you could wind up with a hundred, hundred and ten, hundred and twenty thousand quid at the end of the day.

NICK: Christ!

PAUL: (*Kindly*) Well, in your case perhaps a bit less as you're starting out... But it's not bad, is it? One hundred and twenty grand... If you've got the stamina.

It turns out that Paul finally has not got the 'stamina', and the honour of writing *United Kingdom* passes to Nick Croucher. From this disaster there follows for Paul, as night follows day, despair, madness, an attempt at suicide and the final knell of a part-share in a BAFTA Award.

Yet, watching the Warehouse's production of *Television Times*, it struck me that it was not these dramatic alarms that most nearly touched the heart of the TV writer's blues, whatever it is that makes them on the whole such a wingeing bunch. As Paul was portrayed by Karl Johnson (than whom no actor can more clearly project free-floating anxiety and depression), it was these early scenes that said it best. There sits a man entombed in a plastic cubicle. On the studio floor, so far away it might be miles, the fruits of his creation are being thoroughly worked over by the professionals. He has no serious control over what is happening. All he can do is watch a tiny screen in front of him that blinks on and off in apparently random sequence. From time to time he breaks into a tense and bitter monologue. Occasionally people look in to ridicule and insult him, fire unanswerable questions at him or announce that there's been a strike, a fire, a flood—and whatever it is it will need an extensive rewrite within the next five minutes. The actors are mutinying. The director never liked the script. The producer has flown to Hong Kong. The writer is a fool of fate and miserably paid to boot.

I recognize there is much personal paranoia floating around here, but perhaps some truth too. And I suspect that it is this everyday functional powerlessness that is central to the process that can turn bright young writers into punched-out cynics—much more so than the newsworthy clashes over whether or not he can have his characters say 'fuck' and 'cunt' or flash their pricks in prime time. And I suspect too that this process is built into the system and not easily correctable. Abstinence may be the only answer. The problem is that when it comes to the crunch most TV writers will probably echo the words of the suicidal Paul Prior as, chock-full of Seconal pills, he prepares to go down for the third time: 'Television—I love it!'

Video-Mad: An American Writer in British Television

HOWARD SCHUMAN

I have grown video-mad, for many different reasons and in many different ways. One harmless manifestation: I store my life on a (mental) video cassette which I frequently run on a (metaphysical) machine. When it is wound to the end, I reverse to move forward.

(REVERSE) 1965. HAMBURGER SONGS

I spent most of the sixties on the island of Manhattan, writing for theatres and cabarets: beyond the fringe and on the rocks. Classically broke, I would occasionally collaborate with a friend on dreadful pop songs, pathetic imitations of chart hits, which we flogged to schlock music publishers for fifty dollars. We called them our hamburger songs.

During the era of hamburger songs, I happened to see the BBC/National Theatre *Uncle Vanya* on our local do-gooding educational channel (programmes from the UK were a rare event in 1965). I had long affected to (and perhaps actually did) despise television. But this video Chekhov riveted me. I wondered why a production not especially created for the medium should have more style, fluidity and confidence than anything I had seen on American television for years.

(PAUSE) 1981. LOOSE CONNECTIONS

When I moved to London (late 1968) I began to watch television with an avidity I hadn't felt since *Sgt. Bilko* unhinged my adolescent mind. It became clear that *Vanya* had been a good but not exceptional example of the British mastery of studio/video techniques. A skill

74

even more impressive (to me) when applied to new work, from Potter and Mercer to *Monty Python* and *Coronation Street* (Mike Apted's automobile/bus collision episode, recently reshown, was the Burning of Atlanta in a studio).

My love for British television was sudden and violent and perhaps I expected too much, as lovers do. For it seems (to me, in 1981) that an honourable tradition is withering away as more and more air time is filled with factory products so defective they should never have left the factory floor: US/British imitations of proven genre hits: carbon copies of already smudged originals. The air, in fact, is heavy with hamburger songs.

(FAST FORWARD) 1971. EVERYTHING UP TO 'BUFFALO SHIT' IS TERRIFIC

I came to London with my h.s. partner to work on a 'quality' English musical that never materialized. We were determined to stay in England a while and avoid the traps of American success (which we knew, of course, only by hearsay). After a few months we completed a satirical film which was bought (surprisingly) and never made (not surprisingly). The script, however, fell into the hands of an AIP executive in charge of developing Vincent Price Projects. Sniffing at the trends of the day, the Exec decided that the new Price opus should combine *Monty Python* and *M*A*S*H* and that the young authors of an unproduced satirical film were hungry enough to take him seriously. He handed us a bloody and unpleasant novel about a satanic American actor making a film in England and told us to 'have fun with it'. Our first problem was how to 'have fun' with a series of Black Mass axe murders on Hampstead Heath. We turned the central character into a flamboyant, not awfully bright, washed-up veteran of grade Q horror movies, who is flown to London by a Lew Grade figure to host a campy late-night series of the worst films of all time. The show becomes a cult success, the Lew Grade figure is revealed to be a tool of the Devil (satire), slipping satanic/right-wing propaganda into Price's monologues, and the aging ham actor finds himself spokesperson for a (literally) diabolical fascist political movement. We delivered the script still quietly chuckling to ourselves.

The Executive read it, telephoned to say it was 'some job' but perhaps not quite ready for The Coast so he was sending over a few notes to aid us in getting the script into shape for its journey west.

Twenty-five single-spaced typewritten pages arrived soon after. The first comment was: *Everything up to 'Buffalo Shit' on Page 3 is terrific.* Well: Page 1 consisted of the Credits, Page 2 was a description of a plane landing at Heathrow and Price's expletive 'Buffalo Shit' was the first line of dialogue on Page 3.

My partner and his wife returned to America to seek the traps of American success. I had a go at writing a television play.

(PAUSE) WHY?

Back in America it would have been unthinkable to consider writing for television, that vast mechanism for selling consumer goods. But in England ... for a start there was infinitely more variety offered by the three channels here than the seven in New York. The top 30 per cent of fiction programmes demonstrated a range of content, style, wit, commitment and (occasionally) innovation I hadn't thought possible in the medium. I suspected there were people involved in British television for reasons other than Big Pounds. (When I learned what most writers were paid my suspicion was confirmed.) The excellence of direction and acting was impressive enough but what really staggered me was the breed of 'Television Writer' producing single plays and episodes of series and serials and even the odd sit com (the weakest fiction area) which made the fabled 'Golden Age of American Television' (the fifties) seem more like brass if not dross. Instead of the sentimental family sagas beloved of my countrymen and women, there were compassionate but tough plays like *The Gorge*; in place of contrived 'problem plays' there were works of intellect and complexity like *The Parachute*. To be sure, there was also a mass of sterile, mechanical, even offensive work but it was the acres of good stuff that attracted me. I wanted to work in those fields.

(PLAY) AUTUMN 1971. MOZART IS IRRELEVANT

During the short, cold summer of love in San Francisco (1967), a draft-resisting acid head found me listening to *Don Giovanni* and pityingly informed me that 'Mozart is irrelevant, man.' I was very influenced by this guy at the time: he had (briefly) convinced me that grass and acid and magic mushrooms were the short cuts to a new consciousness but I knew at that moment I would eventually drop out of the counter culture because Mozart was relevant (to me). I was anti-capitalist and pro *Don Giovanni* and if that was a fatal contradiction I would just have to try to deal with it.

Wondering what was happening to my friend and his ideas in the seventies, I had begun to doodle with a stage play which imagined him in London on the run from the draft. But in addition to exploring the evaporation of the best and the worst of sixties 'thinking' I also wanted to write about the conflict between the rampant egos of New York and the controlled egos of London ... chaotic versus structured personalities ... I couldn't make any of this work as a stage play but as I began to think of it as a television play the piece seemed to take off.

It was partly being able to move around more freely. But the final lift-off came from solving a technical problem. The one aspect of British television that irritated me was the arbitrary mix of video and film. Video for indoor (studio) sequences and film for outdoor scenes. Celluloid allows for such subtle gradations of light, and film sound is so much more atmospheric that when intercut with video (a bolder medium which conveys an immediate 'presence' that is, paradoxically, far more unreal than film) the effect is unpleasantly jarring. I decided that my play should only use film when there was a reason integral to the plot. And out of this decision, my central character (Mik) evolved from a draft dodger into an ex-sixties radical, now an apolitical experimental film maker, who is shooting impulsive, random images of London ('this film will be a map of my psyche'); all the characters in the play (*Verité*—as in Cinema Verité) were first seen through the eye of Mik's lens. Mik is taken up by a young English couple and he repays them by bringing every kind of late sixties/early seventies madness into their comfortable Islington nest, thereby dragging the schoolteacher wife screaming into the seventies and then taking the somewhat bloodless upper-middle-class husband back to New York for an 'adrenalin fix', leaving behind only his apocalyptic vision of London (having been offered a contract to make a horror film about a modern Jack the Ripper in Manhattan).

I completed the play in November. My agents and friends were enthusiastic. *Verité* was sent to the BBC with the blessing of a Name Director. I went away on a short holiday convinced that when I returned the gates to television's green pastures would be open. This was not the first time in my life I was to prove over-optimistic.

Howard Schuman

(PAUSE) REALITY SHOWS

'Trite'—BBC
'Overwritten'—Yorkshire
'Too weird for Joe Bloggs'—Thames

Verité circulated and was rejected for eighteen months. I came to understand that the men and women who turned it down were not merely rejecting my play but my idea of reality. To me, Harvey (the sound man who was picking up 'cosmic static' from Jupiter that made him 'real tranquil') and Barbara (the New York divorcee trying to come out of her depression/anxiety via tap-dance therapy) and Carlyle (the ex-Austin Reed salesman and self-declared white witch) may have been written in a heightened manner but they were totally real. My lover, my friends and my agents believed in them as well. But would anyone in power ever agree with this small band of believers? I had no accreditation as a playwright or novelist to support my reality show, which was being judged by people who had no understanding of the sixties, much less of where the seventies were heading. This conflict of reality shows is the most formidable hurdle new writers have to overcome, unless they are producing work in imitation of existing plays and genres. The quality of *Verité* could be debated but it wasn't quite like anything else. And that was the problem.

(FAST FORWARD) 1973. CATCHING FIRE

I was getting desperate. *Verité* and two other short plays were doing the rounds. The rejection letters were more rueful but I seemed no nearer having my work performed; 1972 was a £100 year. (And the Americans who controlled the agency representing me had suggested all clients earning less than £5,000 a year be dropped. Luckily one of my agents asked that I be made a special case. A basket case, no doubt.) I had no work permit (and so couldn't even wait on tables) and my partner in hamburger songs was writing thrillers in Manhattan. Close to emotional zero, I wrote another play. Cracking British television had become an obsession, yet I knew in some dreadful way this was the last piece of work I could produce on speculation.

I finished *A Helping Hand* and with casual optimism my agent sent it to Rob Buckler, script-editor of BBC's Thirty Minute Theatre, as he had, cautiously and with many reservations, praised one of my orbiting plays. After he read it, I was invited to have lunch with him in the *waitress service* restaurant at White City. This, I was assured, was many steps up from a mere meeting in an office or sharing a cup of coffee in the canteen.

It may have been a step up but in the course of lunch I could see it was just going to be a more expensive (for the BBC) way of saying no.

A Helping Hand revolves around a working-class/grammar-school guy, now married to an austere woman of means, who wishes he was playing jazz trumpet instead of working in the City. When he offers refuge to a distraught Liverpudlian pill freak he meets on a bus, his motives appear to be compassionate. But as they talk, it's obvious that he is fascinated, and even envious, of her various breakdowns, as he is too repressed to give vent to his frustration and fury. He begs the pill freak to give him some of her very powerful speed, and as he begins to wreck his wife's Georgian house the terrified neurotic flees. The play alternates between the husband's fabricated explanation of the wreckage to his wife (he, naturally, blames it on the p.f.) and flashbacks to the true story.

Over two very tough BBC rump steaks, Rob goes through the play with me. He likes the characters—particularly Pam the pill freak— the beginning and the ending. Feels the middle sags. I take this in. 'Feels the middle sags'. And I know that he's intending to turn the thing down because of its sagging middle. My mind does a flip. I know this is what must be called the last chance. I'm too old and not cute enough for hustling on the Dilly. I overcome all my boring self-doubt and as strong as I've ever been in defence of my work (heretofore I'd always secretly agreed with any and all criticism) I assure him I can fix the sagging middle: it's a rewrite, a polish. There is no problem here. I must have sounded impressively confident because two days later he called to tell me that he and the producer were buying the play.

Almost simultaneously, my agent was rung by a script-editor from Thames Television (which had been infiltrated by a pile of my work: carried in by a friend of mine who worked at Teddington Studios as a Production Assistant) asking if *A Helping Hand* were still free. When she said the BBC were buying it, his interest moved from moderate to intense and she arranged a meeting for us.

This was the breakthrough. A combination of luck and nerve. Eighteen months of agony and suddenly it seemed so simple, like the breaking of a membrane.

Howard Schuman

I met Andrew Brown, the ebullient New Zealander who was script-editing both an hour and a half-hour drama slot for Joan Kemp Welch at Thames. (There is an assumption—to some extent justified—that unlike theatre directors, television directors do not have the time or ability to work with the author on the literary problems of a script; that function is given to a script-editor unless the producer wants to work directly with the writer.) Andrew bubbled enthusiastically about *Helping Hand* and *Verité* (which he would have bought had there been an opening for an hour play) and said that if I had an idea he liked, he'd commission it. For the first time, someone in authority was actually expressing enthusiasm for my plays. (This was the start of a very creative relationship, one that survived for many years.) Under the influence of Antipodean enthusiasm, white wine, and a hot Bank Holiday sun streaming through the windows of the sitting room (a script-editor had let me *inside his house*), I waxed eloquent about an idea for a play to be called *The Surbiton Kid* which dealt with a Surbiton stockbroker obsessed with country and western music (in almost every play I've written, or have intended to write, since arriving in London there occurs to some degree the theme of American influence on Europe—from pop music to pop psychology). The first image was a fifty-year-old woman in twinset and pearls, a cowboy hat perched precariously on her head, singing 'On Top of Old Smokey'. Andrew stopped me. There was no need to go any further. He'd commission it.

I mentally tap danced through the streets of Fulham on my way home. The dancing stopped the next day when Andrew phoned, a bit sheepish, telling me his Producer would have to hear the idea from my very own lips before the commission could be approved. Up/down, that's the show business.

Driving out to Thames' Teddington Lock studio, a few days later, Andrew did two things to relax me. *One*: he said, 'Don't be afraid of Joan Kemp Welch, she's not as tough as she looks.' *Two*: he said, 'Now I'm sure when *you* tell her the idea she'll like it, but is there any other play up your sleeve . . . just in case.'

I sketched *Censored Scenes from King Kong*: a radical journalist comes out of a mental breakdown obsessed with the idea that before the original film of *King Kong* was censored it contained a sequence in which Kong fucked Fay Wray ('I don't think that's Joan's cup of tea') and *then* I sketched *Captain Video to the Rescue*: an Englishman is forced by his American wife to undergo a video therapy, in which

80

couples photograph each other with home video equipment and dissect the resulting tapes with a psychiatrist at the Cool Tubes Institute ('She might go for that,' he mused).

My first thought when Andrew introduced me to Joan Kemp Welch was relief that she was not as tough as she looked. Because she was a hefty, severe woman who looked, well, pretty tough. There was one pleasantry (she liked *Verité* very much) and then it was down to business and I was on. I described the opening of *The Surbiton Kid*, Andrew forced a laugh but it froze in the ice of Joan's gaze. She was not amused. 'Tell Joan about the video therapy, Howard . . .' At the words 'video therapy' the ice melted. And after a brief description of *Captain Video*, Joan said, '*Now* I'm catching fire.' Imagine a woman who looks something like Bette Davis in *The Nanny* undergoing spontaneous combustion and you'll understand why I almost ended my career with an ill-timed snort of hysterical laughter.

It was only later I discovered that Joan Kemp Welch was one of the most important directors in the brief history of television. She had done much of the early TV Pinter and was a brilliant innovator. Her excitement about *Captain Video* had nothing to do with the characters (who were exceedingly vague at this point) but with the play's visual potential: it would mix black and white video of the couple at home with glossy colour when they were with their psychiatrist, Dr Hessler Tint, at the Cool Tubes Institute. The commission was authorized.

I had rewritten *Helping Hand* and was starting on what was to become *Captain Video's Story* (every play in the half-hour slot had 'Story' in the title to give the viewer the false belief that the plays were somehow linked!) when Andrew rang again and said there was an hour slot suddenly vacant (I didn't ask the undoubtedly grisly details) and he and Joan wanted to go into production with *Verité*.

Now, I'm catching fire.

(FAST FORWARD) SUMMER 1973–SPRING 1975. VIDEO MAD

Andrew had said that a condition of *Verité* being produced was that I make some changes in the text. At first I thought he meant toning the play down and prepared for an agonizing tussle with my conscience but in the event his suggestions all proved to be improvements. They were based on the practical fact that I had asked for too many sets: it would be impossible to contain all of them on our one studio day. This technical limitation meant resetting more scenes in the house of Shirley and Clive (the English couple at the centre of the piece), which had the effect of bringing the madness *to* Shirley and, in fact, strengthening rather than weakening the play.

Piers Haggard was given the second draft to read and very quickly said he wanted to direct it. We had a good first meeting (very good from my point of view because he kept telling me how much he liked the play: after all this time in limbo I simply couldn't get enough enthusiasm from people). It is not unknown for a director to tell a writer how much he likes his or her play just before destroying it. But I was to discover that Piers *really* liked and understood the play; as a bonus, he had ideas for improving it. In my second draft script Shirley, Clive and assorted loons turn up at a viewing theatre to view Mik's film. Piers suggested not showing any footage of the film at this point, but only taking reaction shots of the gang watching it and hearing bits of the sound track—saving the images themselves for the very end of the play, when Shirley is alone in her 'middle-class ghetto' in a state of near breakdown. This worked exceedingly well: casting a retrospective chill on all the tap dancing and high jinks that had gone before.

The making of *Verité* was an unusually happy time: the producer, script-editor, director and actors all seemed to care for the play. Piers encouraged me to come to rehearsals (not usual in television) and like most good directors was not defensive if I had any criticisms (my only real worry was when the actors playing Shirley and Clive got a bit too stuck into exploring the Strindbergian subtext of their relationship at the expense of the comedy).

I thought the mix of 16-mm black and white film with the colour video tape was effective. But the revelation for me was the theatricality of the viewing-room sequence. The room was created mainly out of space and light, it wasn't so much 'real' as an atmosphere. When I watched the completed *Verité* it was that scene which stayed most lingeringly in my mind.

This gut sense of the theatrical possibilities of working with video tape continued with *Captain Video's Story*. Sybil, the American wife, had been redecorating the family home in Clapham but lost interest in the middle, stopped and went back to working on her Joni Mitchell-lish songs in an effort to feel creatively fulfilled. All the scenes in the house took place against a background of peeling wallpaper, and these black and white clumsily shot (on purpose) peeling wallpaper scenes contrasted well with the high tech Cool Tubes Institute shot glossily, in colour. This contrast was not a gimmick: it helped to re-inforce the sense of unease the English husband was experiencing as a video camera poked its nose into his most private moments, even his love making ('Wait a second, the red light is on.... You're not shooting *this* are you?').

Captain Video was not quite as happy an experience as *Verité*. The leading actress's New Zealand accent rather undermined her attempt at New York sounds and the peeling wallpaper was more effective in the studio than on tape, as the wonderfully witty details of the set didn't register on the black and white crudely shot tape (this was a fault in my conception and it taught me when to avoid too much detail and go for space and light). However: the two men were excel-lent and as the play built, the movement between home tapes and the prodding of Dr Hessler Tint ('Pain is Growth') provided some fairly intense comedy. And Derek Fowlds made the husband's unleashing of his pent-up aggression fiercely funny and scary.

Above all I can remember walking around the sets on taping day and absorbing their theatricality, which was not the theatricality of the theatre but something more detached and perhaps more ominous. Television, I guess. I was becoming almost unnaturally attracted to the studio, and with the next play I grew totally besotted.

At the suggestion of Brian Farnham, a young director who had wanted to do *Captain Video*, Mark Shivas commissioned me to write *Censored Scenes from King Kong* for a new series of plays by 'contem-porary' writers (this meant the plays were scheduled for a late-night low-budget slot). The first draft of *Kong* was dredged out of my sub-conscious in ten days. Stephen, the central character, returns to London after an absence of some years (he's been to 'Japan') deter-mined to track down 'the Kong story': for what sinister purpose had the notorious love making scene been censored? This obsession collides with the obsessions of his best friends: a quartet of ex-sixties radicals now in the process of converting a Wapping warehouse into a nightclub.

The idea of the warehouse was another instance of limitation being turned around into a strength. I knew we had very little money to make this production and asked Brian and Mike Porter (our designer) whether we could create a huge warehouse space out of the giant BBC studio itself. They jumped at the idea (literally as I remember—we were all pretty tanked in the steamy atmosphere of the BBC Club). Mike built a small glass model, *Citizen Kane* style to suggest a roof (shot on another camera and superimposed), hung a few sheets and lit them from behind to create windows ... and we had an enormous warehouse set to play around with. Brian had the main characters enter at one point through the great dock doors of the studio, which was a breathtaking entrance. Mike Porter created the nightclub out of air and props and the scenes of Stephen's hallucinatory journey to track down the big story were done with Colour Separation Overlay using pop art collages as backgrounds. (CSO is a process in which actors are photographed against a blue background by a camera which does not pick up the colour blue, while another camera shoots the background, and then the two images are electronically mixed. Effective but frighteningly time-consuming.)

The finished play mixed comedy, satire, songs, melodrama; it was shot and acted in a highly stylized way. It could only have been a video piece. (And it still looks impressive today even though it was rough, shot too quickly and exceptionally cheap: total cost of sets in the area of £300—which included the creative team buying the pop art collages from the artist to pay his fee.) It blew a few people's minds (minds were still being blown in 1973). I was crazy about it; it sent me completely video mad. It broke my heart when the BBC refused to transmit it (see: A Good Bleat).

I wrote five more studio plays in the next fourteen months. (Only one script has ever been made on celluloid; *A Helping Hand* was shifted from tape to film because of a threatened studio strike.) All of the plays have very strong thematic and stylistic links: the central characters are in states of (to put it mildly) extreme mental stress; their stories are punctuated by interludes of film or music or narration. (This may have something to do with my early grounding in revue.) For instance, as the heroine of *Anxious Anne*, an American writer of children's books living in a London mews house, retreats further and further into childhood, her disintegration is charted by a chirpy, Jackanory style narrator ('Anne thought she had been a perfect little *schmuck*'). In *Amazing Stories*, a middle-aged Wimbledon accountant mad for pulp science fiction exorcizes anger/frustration over his family's depressive state by imagining a black and white fifties type sci-fi film in which his wife, son and father-in-law are transformed into vegetables by sinister beings from outer space. (A scientist in the film-within-the-play tells him: 'It's too late to save your family, old man, but it may not be too late to save the rest of Wimbledon.')

Video-Mad: An American Writer in British Television

It was a heady time. I was being paid to explore themes and techniques which attracted me. Even when the final productions were disappointing, I always learned something: scale models in CSO . . . the uses of music in 'straight' drama . . . the mix of stylized dialogue and surrealistic situations to make observations about 'real' life . . . By the winter of 1975 I knew two things (well at least two things): my somewhat quirky imagination was at home in studio-bound video tape . . . and I was now desperate to move the ideas and techniques I'd been playing with on to a larger canvas.

As the heroine in a Gothick novel might write: I was to get much more than I'd bargained for.

But first . . . a good bleat.

(PAUSE) A GOOD BLEAT

There was one shadow over this churningly exciting period: the repeated non-appearance of *Censored Scenes from King Kong*. *Kong* was intended for a series of late-night plays but after four programmes had been taped, the series was axed: a victim of the 10.30 p.m. television curfew imposed during the miners' strike. (We received news of the three-day week as we were rehearsing a number called *The Lights are Going Out all over Europe*.) The Head of Plays, Christopher Morahan, viewed the four shows to decide whether homes could be found for the video orphans. Mark Shivas was told that if we cut five minutes out of our fifty-five minute running time, *Kong* would be given a fifty-minute drama slot. There were no obvious cuts but five comparatively expendable minutes were painfully excised (most of a song and one short but important scene). A year passed and the leaner *Censored Scenes* was still not scheduled. Finally, over a veal piccata, Shivas confessed that *Kong* was unlikely ever to see the light of day as Morahan disliked it intensely ('Camp rubbish like *The Rocky Horror Show*') and there was nothing he or I could do about it.

With his permission I wrote to the critics who had praised *Verité* and outlined the situation; Philip Purser and Peter Fiddick asked in print why *Kong* had not been shown but the BBC chiefs chose not to respond (after all, I was a new and unknown-ish author, not newsworthy). *Kong* was kept alive by a bit of good luck: the editor of the theatre magazine *Gambit* was planning a television issue, read the text and decided to publish it. (I once had a letter from a lecturer in media at a Melbourne polytechnic. It seems he'd been teaching *Kong* from the *Gambit* text for a number of years; every semester he discovered that his students puzzled over the same points and he had come up with some pretty cosmic interpretations of the play in trying to answer their questions. He relayed his readings and asked me to confirm or deny them. I had to inform him that, in all honesty, the ambiguities he and his students had been foxed by were due to typographical errors.)

Kong was censored for aesthetic rather than overtly political reasons (but 'aesthetic' judgements in television are frequently political). It offended one man and so a highly original work, designed with great imagination (and on the cheap with many lessons for other designers), acted and directed with commitment and zest, was stored away (although, interestingly, it was not wiped but placed in the BBC vaults). When it had a public showing at the 1977 Edinburgh Television Festival it was very well received. Morahan (no longer Head of Plays) found he had to justify his 1974 decision. He wrote to the *Guardian* saying that if I hadn't been seeking publicity I would have gone to him and talked the matter over. His door, he claimed in disingenuous avuncular fashion, had always been open. Hmm. What I knew of him was not calculated to send me knocking on his door. My first encounter with the man himself was enough to unsettle me permanently: on the first *Kong* taping day I decided to eschew my normal blue denim outfit in favour of something more festive. So I decked myself out in cheap £5 imitation *Great Gatsby* trousers and a sweater into which the legend 'Pain Is Growth' had been knitted (a prop left over from *Captain Video's Story*). When Morahan was introduced to me in the gallery he eyed me up and down through half-closed lids and whispered: 'Well, you look exactly the way I pictured you,' and walked away. Therefore, when Shivas told me that in his opinion there was no point in trying to debate Morahan's decision, I had every reason to believe him.

Kong's fate was painful to accept. But the reason it never surfaced has a larger implication than one author's misery. Christopher Morahan was far from a reactionary right-wing cartoon: not only were many fine plays produced during his regime, but he fought against the banning of several programmes. Unfortunately for me he didn't like my work but others did (including the highly respected Shivas) and it should have been possible for me to fight back. But there was no mechanism by which I could do so. As in so many other aspects of

Video-Mad: An American Writer in British Television

British society, a paternalistic decision had been taken behind closed doors (even so prestigious a writer as Dennis Potter was never given a satisfactory explanation for the banning of *Brimstone and Treacle*).

Amusingly (not really: but I'm trying to be British about all this *Angst*), after *Kong* was favourably reviewed at the Edinburgh Television Festival, James Cellan Jones (Morahan's successor) approved its transmission and Shaun Sutton (Head of Drama) supported him (claiming he had never seen the play in the first place). They then proceeded to schedule its transmission the night before a stage version was to open in London. We asked for a postponement but were told this was the only night it could be transmitted (after four years!). Since the BBC no longer owned the rights I had the option of blocking the transmission and, at the behest of the producer, director and cast of the theatre production, I exercised it. (Shaun Sutton supposedly sighed, 'You just can't win', which I would have thought was my line.) Ken Trodd explained this strange sequel to me: 'You see, the BBC can never forgive anyone they've wronged.'

At the end of a censorship discussion at the Television Festival, which had included a most moving, rather dignified, cry of pain from Dennis Potter (who had been unable to write for a year after the *Brimstone* affair), an IBA official made this pronouncement to the gathering: 'Well, you've all had a really good bleat but that's the way the system is and that's the way it's going to remain.'

Not quite. Following various highly publicized bannings of completed work, the cancellation while in rehearsal of a play by Ian McEwan, and the refusal to sell the controversial *Law and Order* series abroad, even the conservative don't-make-waves Writers' Guild protested so strongly that an early warning censorship mechanism was agreed upon. This is certainly an improvement over what some of us have faced (or have not been allowed to face) in the past. But the BBC–Writers' Guild Agreement only applies to a project that is in production or has been taped. There is no way of fighting against a decision to reject a play/series/serial because of its language or politics or sexual content. Within both the BBC and the ITV companies there is more and more reluctance to tackle contentious scripts: despite a few sparks in the stodge (*Muscle Market*, *Psy Warriors*, *History Man*, etc.) television drama has become almost comprehensibly anodyne. Perhaps there is a shortage of bold writing but the more likely reason is to be found in the escalating conservative pressure on decision makers: the baleful Whitehouse influence

87

(which is alert to Potterion blasphemy but not the shameful racism of a *Mind Your Language*), the advertisers' demand for high ITV ratings (and in response the frightening increase in mindless BBC ratings' fodder), the eye of the government on Television Centre (can the banning of *Scum* and the reluctance to repeat *Law and Order* be unrelated to the fact that the Wilson government put the Corporation under the jurisdiction of the Home Office—an event which deserves a chapter, if not a book, to itself?).

In the face of these pressures, most television decision-makers have behaved with total consistency: they almost always collapse. Decisions are being made behind doors which are not just closed but locked and bolted.

(REVERSE) 1974/1975.
THE SHOW BUSINESS/THE ROCK MUSIC

Another novelty for an American watching British television (in addition to quality) was the concept of the three-, six-, or twelve-part play. In America, television fiction was divided between the one-off play (a fairly extinct breed by the mid-sixties) or the infinite series. (This changed with the success of *Roots* and the coining of the phrase 'mini-series': once there was a name and a category for it, the previously unacceptable idea of a *long play in different parts* became acceptable.) Even before selling *Verité* I was intrigued by the idea of trying to write a six-part play; after *Kong* was taped I began to have serious discussions with Andrew Brown about expanding some of its themes and stylistic devices into a longer work.

One of the most important strands in *Censored Scenes from King Kong* has to do with a highly speedy man attempting, by sheer force of will, to turn a sensitive woman novelist and a Marxist–feminist Ph.D. into a cabaret act. By shifting the ground from cabaret in Wapping to the area of rock music, and by making the women actresses, I felt that the subject could be treated in an equally comic but less surrealistic manner. The idea of a man manufacturing a female rock group seemed ripe with possibilities: for what it could say both about male/female relationships in a macho-dominated industry and also about the change from the rock idealism of the sixties (as it appeared to my generation) to the seventies' trivialization of rock music into yet another plastic branch of show business. I wanted to make use of songs to comment on the action as we had done in *Kong* and to find a studio-based style that would have the flavour of Hollywood movies of the thirties and forties.

Andrew was interested and we began to meet periodically to discuss the project. It was after seeing a gaggle of Busby Berkeley musicals at the National Film Theatre that he came up with one of the key ideas that shaped what would eventually evolve into *Rock Follies*. Whereas *Kong* echoed grade-B melodramas, he felt our plays should refer back to the *Gold Digger* series. The more I thought about it, the more excited I became. First of all . . . it would be fun. Secondly it was a useful touchstone: despite the wild numbers and contrived plots, many of Berkeley's thirties' musicals were firmly set in a Depression context, and I wanted the desperation for rock and roll fame in Project X to be seen against Britain's worsening economic situation. By trying to get the feeling of an old musical into our rock plays, we would be (subliminally) comparing two Depressions and, in a shorthand way, would be saying that most mid-seventies rock bands were simply trying to climb up that old show biz stairway. To make the parallel clear we decided that my two women had to be three women: based on the archetypes of Ruby Keeler, Ginger Rogers and Aline MacMahon. It was a question of style dictating content.

Strangely, this ambitious and, for television, off-beat project (TV decision makers hate to mix their categories: music should mean light entertainment not drama) was commissioned very easily. Verity Lambert was made Head of Drama at Thames Television. She had worked with Andrew and she liked the two plays of mine she knew: when I said I wanted to write a six-part play about women, rock music and failure, she asked if the emphasis would be on personal relationships rather than on the technical details of the rock industry; I said yes and she agreed to commission a first script. I wrote it fairly quickly and it was dismal; however, a second draft was more successful and in February 1975 Verity informed me she was giving the go-ahead to our project, now entitled *Rock Follies*.

(FAST FORWARD) AUGUST 1975/ APRIL 1977. ROLLER COASTER

We're on a roller coaster
And there isn't any turning back . . .
('Roller Coaster', *Rock Follies*, Episode 5)

Dee, Q and Anna, the three central *Rock Follies* women, are actresses who meet when they are cast in a doomed revival of a thirties American musical called *Broadway Annie*. I had placed the rehearsals for this epic in the Latvian Hall but Andrew and Verity thought that too surreal a notion and prevailed upon me to change the venue, which I did—to a Boy Scouts' club. I was therefore delighted to be told that real life rehearsals for the series would be held in the Serbian Community Centre, Ladbroke Grove. (Clive James commented many years later that even when the details of the scripts were at their most imaginative, they were still accurate.)

Rehearsals began in August: the next six months were marked by terror and exhilaration. The reasons for terror were fairly obvious: we were attempting to produce a six-part picaresque musical/drama (in which the drama was as important as the music) on a low budget and with only twelve days per fifty-minute segment (and our directors had only been allocated two studio days for each episode, the same as a straight play—this proved to be impossible and many 'pick up' days were added to our schedule). The leading actresses (Julie Covington, Charlotte Cornwell and Rula Lenska) had to learn three new songs per episode, master David Toguri's choreography, forge their characters, pre-record the songs ... Andy Mackay had to compose the music and arrange it with our resident 'Little Ladies' band, at the same time he worked with Roxy Music in real life ... and because the plays were literally a journey, the scripts called for many sets, costumes, dozens of major and minor characters (and every character conceived as a comic cameo, no matter how brief his or her actual screen time). All this in the context of a series that was breaking the rules of television drama by mixing (like *King Kong*) the serious, the satiric, the comic with extended musical sequences. There was one other small problem: the scripts weren't finished. On our first day of rehearsal only three out of six scripts were completed and I wasn't at all sure of what was going to happen in the last three segments (although, strangely, I'd known for some time that the final incarnation of my actresses turned female rock group would be as a sub-Andrews Sisters outfit singing in a nightclub dedicated to World War II austerity, which would be called The Blitz and would, in the end, be itself blitzed by an explosion—the cause of this explosion as yet a mystery to me). I had been late starting Episode 2—because of my commitments to write *Amazing Stories* and *Anxious Anne*—but I finished it in four weeks, which cheered Andrew up, and then I became completely stuck in 'The Road' episode which eventually took almost three months to finish—an impossibly long time for a television series, even though I thought of it as a long play. The actual writing of the scripts and lyrics for the next three episodes was a good example of the terror/exhilaration cycle: much of the second half of *Rock Follies* was shaped by the playing of the actors (Julie's strength and singing power made Dee the motor of the group, the chemistry between Dee and David (Chris Neal), her young groupie, made his reappearance inevitable, Rula's vulnerability forced me to deepen Q's character, etc., etc.). On the other hand when I again became stuck in Episode 5, knowing that a script delay could cost thousands and thousands of pounds, I was physically sick on more than one occasion. It became clear that there are certain basic differences in temperament required for the writing of a single play and the writing of a series. I am by nature a slow, boringly neurotic playwright (galvanized for a five-year stretch into being prolific) who is strongly attracted to the larger canvas of the six- and twelve-part play. I found out many years later from Verity Lambert that Andrew despaired at one point of my being able to complete *Rock Follies* alone and wanted to call in another writer—in the end I was saved by two strikes, which gained me an extra four weeks.

Despite these terrors, there was a sense, almost from the first read-through, that something special was happening. The chemistry between the scripts, the lyrics, the music, the design, the movement, direction, and the actors felt right. Actors who joined the company, even if just for a short scene in one episode, all seemed to pick up the vibe. We were a Unit.

This happens very rarely on a studio-based series (as opposed to a filmed series where an identity is forged more easily). It occurred on *Rock Follies* for many reasons: almost everyone was aware that good or bad, the series was breaking new ground in its mix of styles, in its use of music, the earthiness of language and situation; it belonged to a generation conditioned by the sixties. The personalities and skills of the directors complemented one another: Brian Farnham was particularly good at helping actors build performances; Jon Scofield was an excellent *editor* of performances and his use of video tape was breathtaking. He was able to cut in his head, the way a Hitchcock worked with celluloid. Jon knew instinctively when to shoot a scene with elaborate editing effects and when simply to let a single camera roll on two good actors. Having been a designer he was able to help Rod Stratfold and Alex Clarke realize the visions in Andrew's head and mine, emphasizing light and space suggestion over literal details (thereby cementing for me many of my own notions about television design).

No matter how good the chemistry of the creative team, there could have been no Unit if we weren't being protected by Verity Lambert and Jeremy Isaacs, Controller of Programmes. They had to fend off members of the Board who hated the scripts, they had to back Andrew up when we needed more studio time, and more money, and support him in trying to keep the most talented and committed cameramen, lighting designers, sound engineers and vision mixers working on the team, rather than accept the normal pot-luck rota system whereby the technicians assigned to an episode may be totally out of sync with the spirit of the series. This protection extended to questions of script censorship. Verity and Jeremy convinced the resident IBA overseer that since *Rock Follies* was satirical it needed a certain latitude in its use of language, drugs references, etc. The censor stepped in once: the 'Little Ladies' have agreed to appear in a soft-porn musical, the featured stud asks the director how many orgasms he wants. I was asked to replace the word 'orgasm' which the censor found distasteful. I rewrote the sentence to read: 'Why can't I just grease up my pectorals and poke her one, you know the usual?' This was passed (presumably as being in excellent taste).

When Verity looked at a rough assembly of the first part of Episode 3, she was pleased and began to talk about a follow-up series. At first the idea horrified all of us in the inner sanctum, as we already were exhausted. But when *Follies* finally appeared and it became a talking point, highly controversial (especially because of the language: a taxi driver said to me 'I was watching with my Mum and she turned to me and yelled, "You can't say *wank* on television", and I said to her "Well, they just fucking did, luv"'), garnering much critical acclaim and very respectable ratings for a drama series (even though it never made the ratings first time around) and (astonishingly) the album of songs which had been recorded (very quickly for £12,000) became the number one album in the country (without any radio play) . . . it became clear that the roller coaster ride was not over. Cynics were to write that the overriding reason for the sequel was that Andrew Brown, Andy Mackay and myself were out to make a packet. This demonstrated a considerable ignorance about the toll an RF takes on your nervous system, the fact that Andrew Brown had no financial stake in the series, and that if money was my my primary goal I could have accepted the £250,000 I was offered to write an Americanized version.

Enough pleading. The sequel stands or falls by itself. For me the main justification for writing it was to experiment by telling more of the story through music—without turning it into a standard musical—and by creating a simpler plot line around the internal pressures among the women, rather than a struggle between Us (the 'Little Ladies') and Them (the record business). I also wanted to write in a woman manager—which would have the effect of focusing the drama on women rather than on women and men. I felt that it might be a very long time before there would be another chance to mix music and drama on such an elaborate scale (unfortunately, this instinct was absolutely correct). Although RF2 was created in a more self-conscious atmosphere (because we were following up a known quantity) to the degree that at one point our rehearsals were even filmed for a documentary ... the sense of Unit prevailed (with Bill Hays replacing Jon, who felt he had done it all once).

If anything, the work in the studio was even more committed second time around. The powerful sense of involvement was typified by one particular event. Bill Hays was directing the 'Looney Tunes' episode, in which all the central characters are experiencing extreme paranoia (sexual, political and musical). There have been snatches of a sort of paranoia anthem called 'Looney Tunes' all through the episode but it is only sung in full near the end of the play. Bill was seeking an effect that would top the ones that had gone before (in which the singers were dressed in pastel clown suits and photo-graphed in a fairground distorting mirror), when an anonymous technician called down to the gallery and suggested that the vision mixer press a certain sequence of buttons, at which point Julie Covington and Derek Thompson (who were being photographed at the time) seemed to disappear until all that was left of them were a few black lines which made them look like two connect-me-dot drawings: the perfect visualization of their characters' wish to disappear from the heaviness oppressing them. I think that moment sums up the best of the *Rock Follies* experience: a magnetic field of energy was fre-quently created in rehearsal room and studio that attracted mental contributions from actors, designers, directors and technicians alike.

When I was high (and not throwing up or under the covers with psychogenic sinus headaches) I felt: television could be like this all the time. The show business could be like this all the time. The

93

feeling was intense while it lasted. But it didn't last long. After the third episode of the second series was transmitted, *Rock Follies of '77* went off the air for six months. There was a Production Assistants' strike and the last three episodes could not be edited. There were many complicated issues involved and labour relations were never particularly healthy at Thames. I thought it was ironic, however, that the only television series with a left-wing viewpoint, one that was going to end with a critique of the Silver Jubilee celebrations at a time of high unemployment (and make that statement on the very Royal Anniversary day itself!), was allowed by the unions to go off the air (to the relief of some members of Management). Even worse to me was the fact that neither of our Production Assistants had the grace to ring me up and say they regretted what had happened. The result of the strike was that the public never saw the second series as intended—how damaging this was only became clear in October 1980, when the National Film Theatre showed both series over a single weekend. Dozens of people wrote to say they had never realized that the second series was not only funny but quite moving/disturbing. Who could blame them: it was as if the audience at a new play was asked to wait six months between Acts I and II.

When the second series was virtually destroyed by the PA strike, the intensity of my joy evaporated. And the real life took over with a vengeance.

(FAST FORWARD) WINTER 1978/ WINTER 1979. NORMAL HUMAN PROBLEMS

I had an idea for another long play (see: She was a Dream) but I knew it was a good idea to get out of television for at least eighteen months by which time I was sure my enthusiasm would return. I had an exceedingly good time (not easy but satisfying) working on the stage version of *Censored Scenes from King Kong* (relishing the luxury of theatre rehearsal time, even on the fringe, for sculpting/rewriting a script, even if it does allow the actors more time to display/indulge in their traumas of distrust and self-doubt—as well as happier displays of bravery and faith).

After *Kong* I should probably have written another theatre piece but instead I decided to spend an experimental year in the Movie Business. (You fool! Don't do it ... turn back...) I had been approached by two bouncy independent producers (a team I came to think of as D&C) to write a film of *Follies*. This was not the first such offer and I said no yet again. Was there anything I would like to write? I admitted (please ... please don't do it!) that I knew a local band in Pimlico whose manager worked out of a record store and I had become emotionally involved in their struggle to be part of the New Music Renaissance that seemed to be happening in the wake of Punk: the return to spare music, the small venues, the mini-record companies competing with the multinationals, etc. D&C brightened up: it could be like *Car Wash* only different. A look at London and the new Rock Music with me writing script and lyrics, Andy Mackay composing the music ... a cinematic *Follies* for the end of the seventies ...

Telling myself it was an experiment and that my eyes were wide open and I'd be returning to television ... I sweated the poisons out of my system at a Health Farm and started my screenplay.

It took four months before the characters came to life ... D&C were supportive and enthusiastic (even though the few completed pages horrified them—the work was stupid and dead, in the great tradition of all my first drafts; I also realized I was crazy attempting another ambitious original after five years of intensive writing). However: by the summer a script had been forged and we all agreed it was promising. It centred around two male friends (not-gay): the Talent (Singer-Composer, a working class version of a Woody Allen neurotic) and the Drive (Eddie Boffey, the hustler, operating—like his much nicer original—out of a record store and fantasizing success in a few stylized numbers set in The Eddie Boffey Theatre of the Mind). D&C made some sensible critical comments, I did a polish and a few months later—to my amazement, and I think theirs— United Artists said they would commit three million dollars to the project, which was to be made in London, with a cast of unknowns, and a British director to be mutually agreed upon.

In my euphoria I lost the detachment I had been cultivating (this 'just an experiment') and also my wariness. I figured that since the bread had been promised on the basis of my original script, and that the director would be British (not a nasty, ruthlessly ambitious *Yank*), the finished film might at least resemble my screenplay.

(Pause for the cosmic laughter to die down.)

I will make the rest of the tale as short as it was inevitable. A Young

Respected Television Film Director was selected (with my approval). I was eager to write another draft: I thought of the script as it stood only as a blueprint for a livelier and more cinematic film. But after six weeks of meetings, it seemed to me that an awful melodrama was emerging. ('That's *Drama*' the YRTFD would shout, as he suggested yet another bit of sexual soap opera.) I felt I could fend off the soap operatics . . . but out of the blue came The Beginning of the End. We had started to audition singer/actors based on the first draft. One of the characters was a woman sax player—she calls herself Velvet Trulls and claims to be an eighteen-year-old from Hackney but is revealed to be twenty-four-year-old Rose Kaplan, daughter of a right-wing gynaecologist from Highgate. A singer called Lena Lovich auditioned for the part, was absolutely perfect, and we decided to offer her Velvet/Rose when and if UA gave the project the final green light. That night YRTFD called and said that when he imagined Lena reading the part of Darryl (The Talent), the part came to life in a way it never had done before (for him). I pointed out this little problem: Darryl was a guy. 'No, he's not. You don't realize it but you've written a woman. His idealism, his vulnerability . . . those are feminine characteristics . . .' I called a meeting between me, YRTFD and D&C. I calmly offered to leave the project: there was no point in arguing the commercial pros and cons of making Darryl into Darrylette or whatever . . . he was a guy and I was not putting him through a sex change operation. C agreed with me saying it was a perfectly idiotic idea but D (the female half) thought it was a brilliant concept, one that would give the film some 'normal human problems'. By which she meant sex, presumably. I replied that the script was already about the death of capitalism, urban violence, the rise of fascism, and the betrayals of friendship (in addition to being pretty funny), and I thought those were quite enough problems for one film. I stood my ground, repeating my (perfectly sincere) offer to resign. I was assured that no one else could write the film, it was in my own very wonderful and unique style . . . etc. D drove me home . . . 'You're really sure about this woman thing . . . ?' I was. I then suffered through a horrendous stint attempting to produce a second draft in the teeth of my certainty that the work was necessary but in all probability futile. Sure enough. I completed the second draft, went away for a week, and when I came back my agent said, 'They think it's terrific but that it would be even more totally terrific if the central character were a woman.' At this point I asked her to relay to all three of them, that they severally and individually get stuffed (or words to that effect).

The most important point about this detour is that by April 1979, I couldn't wait to return to television to work with Andrew on a project for Verity back at Thames, the Mother Ship.

(FAST FORWARD) MARCH 1980.
SHE WAS A DREAM

Since June 1977, an idea for a series had been gestating in what was left of my mind. It was to be called *The Ann Lovington Hour*. Designed as a twelve-hour epic, *Ann Lovington* was centred around a funny, observant twenty-two-year-old from Billericay (Janet Vera Cunningham) full of self-doubt and totally dependent on other, stronger people (mainly women) to motivate her. She is persuaded (with great reluctance) to break out of the mental paralysis that is preventing her from making a life in London. Jan leaves the security of family and married life, arrives friendless in North Kensington and becomes sexually and politically involved with a wide variety of characters. Each hour is devised to be partly shot on film, on location (a 'reality show' about Jan's adventures in North London), and partly shot in a highly stylized way in the studio (a 'dream show' with a separate plot line in which Jan imagines herself as Ann Lovington, internationally successful artist and a highly effective political personality). For the first nine hours, the dividing line between reality and imagination would be firm, the two states treated as two different television programmes. But when Jan's community erupts in rioting (this was being written long before Brixton and Toxteth, by the way), the emotional screw turns painfully and reality and dream become almost indistinguishable (this was to be visualized in television terms; in the ninth episode, for instance, the stylized credits for the Dream Show would appear only minutes into the Reality Show).

It was, natch, not easy to crack the scripts. But by the autumn of 1979, Andrew and I felt the series was on the right tracks. So did Verity Lambert who had commissioned them ... but our personal reality show was beginning. Our protection was evaporating (the way they say the earth's ozone layer is being worn away): Jeremy Isaacs had left after a Boardroom Struggle to be replaced by Bryan 'Ginger'

Cowgill, ratings genius, late of the BBC. I believe *Ann Lovington* could have weathered this sea change, even though we had been very much counting on Jeremy to protect our anti-monetarist, anti-Tory political stance (it is the axing of funds to a Black Community Centre that precipitates the street violence). The final nail in Ann's coffin (although I only came to appreciate this in retrospect) was Verity's move from Head of Drama at Teddington to Head of Euston Films, which meant she no longer had anything officially to do with the series. Her successor, John Frankau, at first seemed to like the project. Then he indicated he didn't actually 'dig it' but would support it. Then in December 1979, he wrote a memo to Andrew: 'I have read the first three scripts, the reality show has all the reality of a wet dream on St Swithin's Day, the dream show is, of course, a night-mare and the politics so extreme and the language so offensive I feel we should immediately send the script to John Bidell [the IBA's resident censor]. But Bryan Cowgill assures me you know what you're doing . . .'

At this point, Andrew and I were legally entitled to pull out. Had I seen the memo at the time it was written I would have insisted we leave and go to the BBC (by some accident Graeme MacDonald, Head of Series and Serials, had slots available for us). But Andrew received assurances from Bryan Cowgill that as long as we cut the series down from twelve episodes to ten (all the ITV companies were claiming financial difficulties after an autumn strike) *Ann Lovington* would live.

We had a director, designers were being considered, casting was underway . . . I had to go to New York for the American production of *Censored Scenes from King Kong* . . . I flew back to London in the middle of rehearsals with the fourth dream show rewritten and the fifth reality show, both of which Andrew approved . . . I returned to Manhattan and then, six weeks before the projected read-through, Andrew arrived to tell me that Cowgill was now saying that unless we cut the series down to eight episodes it was off. I assumed this was an idle threat to try to save money on a very adventurous, potentially contentious series. I pointed out there was no way to cut two more hours out of *Lovington*, it would be tight enough trying to do it in ten. But Andrew said they weren't messing about . . . he reckoned they wanted to kill it and this was the way out. A few weeks later he called from London, in tears, and said *Ann* was dead at Thames.

Video-Mad: An American Writer in British Television

Our catch phrase for the show was 'She's A Dream'. Roger Bamford, the director, packed up his office and then wrote in aerosol on the wall: She *Was* A Dream.

After a legal argy bargy Andrew (legally co-creator of the show) and I got the rights back.

Graeme MacDonald paid for the scripts. He would give us a final yes or no in November but he was confident of steering the series through the BBC decision-making machinery. But the delay was to prove fatal. By November I felt Andrew's head was too deeply into another project (a film he was writing and producing) and he, in turn, lost faith in my ability to write the scripts well enough or fast enough. In the same week that the BBC committed over one million pounds to *The Ann Lovington Hour*, Andrew Brown officially resigned from the project. Stunned, Graeme MacDonald postponed the series for a year. The decision as to its future passed to his successor David Reid, who felt that the plays 'didn't work'. He was especially disturbed by the reality show which to him wasn't real at all. So in March 1981, I was being told the same things I had been told back in 1972. The conflict in reality shows is clearly permanent.

(STOP) 1981. WHAT DO YOU DO FOR A LIVING, JACK-O?

I wrote an article for *New Society* magazine in 1977: 'The Bovril of the Masses'. I said that broadly speaking the television industry was divided between those who felt that programmes should pacify viewers (conceiving the medium as a kind of electronic Bovril) and those who wanted to engross (the original meaning of entertain) rather than distract the audience . . . who wanted to make them high with laughter or speedy with anger . . . who wanted joyous acclaim or excited arguments in sitting rooms after a programme was over . . .

I'd like to make people high, angry, excited . . . all those things. When I was interviewed at the National Film Theatre and a guy stood up and told me my work was reactionary crap I wasn't happy exactly but my adrenalin pumped in the way it wouldn't if I'd been told: 'I think your work is quite nice, dear' . . .

But I've been out of the industry four years. My telephone isn't buzzing with offers. (Although there is a chance that Central will make *Ann Lovington* for the new fourth channel.) Without the protection of executives like Jeremy Isaacs and Verity Lambert ... here is the reality show in all bleak objective fact: a writer doesn't own the means of production (what an insight, get that down!) and if he (or she) is going to write in quirky ways, then he (or she) is going to need more than a little help from his (or her) friends.

I also find, with rare exceptions, I am totally out of tune with the drama output (especially ITV's but also the BBC—with a few exceptions like *Muck and Brass* the glorious *Private Schulz*). So much air time is taken up with hamburger songs. A few months ago I was boggled by the first scene of a BBC-1 *Bouquet of Barbed Wire*-ish (*très manqué*) series.

Time: early morning.
Place: bedroom of a mock-Tudor house in deepest Fantisurrey.
Husband, ready for business, in grey pin-stripe.
Wife, still abed, in pink frillies.
Husband sits on bed. Wrestling, nuzzling, *doubles entendres* follow.
And then, this remarkable expository monologue from the Wife:

> You know, Jack-O, we've been married for two and a half years, ever since my first husband died, and you took me around the world for a year and you've been looking after me and Tom, my son by my first husband, and we live in this lovely house and we have a live-in maid and two smashing cars ... and I still don't know what you do for a living.

This is only a marginally unfair paraphrase. Perhaps my sight and sound are being impaired by bile but the Wife's monologue seems to epitomize what the video decision-makers are looking for at the moment. If I'm right in this feeling ... then I can't help wondering what I'm going to do for a living, Jack-O.

Word into Image: Reflections on Television Dramatization

HUGH WHITEMORE

Those Tories who regard the television industry as a hotbed of leftish egalitarianism should take comfort from the fact that during the past twenty years or so, the tiny, enclosed world of TV drama has managed to create for itself a remarkably rigid structure of class distinctions. At the top are the aristocrats of the single play, then come those who work on prestige serials, followed by the manufacturers of popular series, with soap opera labourers languishing at the bottom. Somewhere in the middle—the equivalent of skilled plumbers, perhaps, or electrical engineers—are those who make dramatizations and adaptations. In a recent issue of the magazine *Gambit*, Tom Stoppard referred to his television version of *Three Men in a Boat:* 'When it's something like that,' he said, 'you're more a craftsman than an artist. I think it's right to take pride in one's craftsmanship as much as one's originality.' Bravo, Tom! Because *Tinker, Tailor, Soldier, Spy* or *Testament of Youth* seems to translate so effortlessly from the page to the screen, the work of adaptors like Arthur Hopcraft or Elaine Morgan often tends to be ignored—or worse, taken for granted. This is particularly deplorable because the high standard of television dramatizations has been one of the most cheeringly consistent features of British TV for the past two or three decades.

What, then, is the nature of this craft? Since every book or short story creates its own problems for the dramatist, and since writers go about their task in widely differing ways, the best I can do is to offer a few instances from my own experience in the hope that they will throw some light on to the process by which a work of prose becomes adapted into a television film or play.

Early in the 1970s, the Granada producer Derek Granger decided that he wanted to do a number of dramatizations of short stories

101

about English country life between the wars; the series was to be called *Country Matters*. After reading material by such writers as David Garnett, D. H. Lawrence and Llewellyn Powys, Granger focused his attention on two authors: H. E. Bates and A. E. Coppard. He then began his search for suitable dramatists.

When I was told about the project, I hoped to be offered a story by Coppard, whose literary reputation made him rather more attractive—or so I thought. In fact, Granger sent me a story by H. E. Bates: *Breeze Anstey*. For me, the first reading of source material is of crucial importance. I have learned to obey the voice of instinct; and on the rare occasions when I have overruled myself, I have always regretted it. I remember, for instance, being sent a story by the distinguished film director, Fred Zinnemann. Although I found it interesting, I was unable to respond to the material with whole-hearted enthusiasm. Nevertheless, because of my desire to work with Mr Zinnemann, I accepted the job. The script that I wrote, although technically competent, lacked conviction and creative vitality—and, quite rightly, I was replaced by another writer. My bruised ego was somewhat comforted by the knowledge that my first instinct had been proved right: I was indeed the wrong man for the job. For unless a writer can approach a dramatization with the same energy and vigour that he brings to an original work, the project can never develop satisfactorily. This does not mean that a writer should restrict himself to one particular type of dramatization; on the contrary, I have found it very stimulating to work with many different genres, using the widest range of source material. But the initial response to this material must always be strong and positive.

To return to *Breeze Anstey*: as soon as I read it, I knew that it could make a wonderful television film. It was visually atmospheric, with two well defined leading characters and an intriguing, understated eroticism. Briefly, the story concerns two girls—Lorn Harvey and Breeze Anstey—who leave their suburban homes to establish a small herb farm. As time passes, their relationship becomes increasingly intimate, with Breeze developing a profound, but unexpressed, lesbian passion for Lorn. Eventually, Lorn's lover, a man of middle-age, returns from overseas and destroys the idyll.

I agreed to attempt the dramatization and was provided with two items of preliminary intelligence: the story would be filmed entirely on location, and the director would probably be Peter Wood.

Having read and studied the original text, I put it aside and, as always, wrote the first draft from memory, as if it were my own story. In my experience, this rather arrogant assumption of authorship is an essential part of the process of dramatization. I find that it gives me more creative energy and injects an element of risk and excitement into what might become a mechanical transposition from one medium to another. Only for the final draft do I return to the book to check details of speech and characterization.

The Bates story is extremely condensed, and begins after the two girls have arrived at their new home in the country. I felt that it would be more effective dramatically if the film were to open with the girls' departure from the suburbs (thus sketching in their social background), and then to continue with their journey to the farm. This, I thought, would give the opening section of the film an appropriate sense of movement as well as providing the director some good opportunities for visual story-telling. The sequence I drafted showed Lorn and Breeze loading their car and saying goodbye to Lorn's parents, who quite clearly regarded the whole enterprise with some anxiety and disapproval. Later, it was decided that Lorn's parents should be Welsh—'It'll make them countryfied but not too heavy,' said Derek Granger. This new opening, with its hint of abduction and frowned-on adventure, set the mood for the main sweep of the film.

Opening sequences always demand the greatest care; no matter how ingenious and sensitive an adaptation may be, it can be utterly destroyed if the first few moments do not capture the essence of what is to follow. Even in conventional narrative drama an opening sequence can pose tricky problems. For some considerable time I was at a loss to know how to cope with the beginning of Daphne du Maurier's *Rebecca*, with its famous first sentence, 'Last night I dreamt I went to Manderley again.' One solution would be to have it spoken as a voice-over narration by Miss du Maurier's unnamed heroine, but this seemed dull and unimaginative. (It had also been done before, by Robert E. Sherwood and Joan Harrison in their screenplay for the Hitchcock film.) Finally, I devised a scene in which the heroine, approaching middle age, was seen recounting her dream to an unidentified listener; as she spoke, so the picture dissolved into her memory, and the story proper began. The director, Simon Langton, developed this device with pleasing subtlety: he suggested that the scene should be set in a room that hinted at a Continental location—a hotel suite in France, perhaps, or on the

Italian Riviera—thus enlarging on an idea in the closing pages of the book when Colonel Julyan advises Maxim de Winter: 'Take a short holiday. Go abroad perhaps.' In this way the element of mystery was immediately introduced into the viewer's mind, creating exactly the right mood for the story that was to follow.

A small footnote to *Rebecca*: Miss du Maurier's refusal to name her heroine created a host of minor difficulties. How, for example, could we dramatize the scene in which the unnamed girl introduces herself to Maxim de Winter? Since the simplest solutions are invariably the best, I wrote a sequence in which the introduction took place entirely in long shot, in a hotel lounge, with the actors' voices drowned by the chatter of passing guests and the sedate music of a Palm Court trio.

Apart from such technical trivialities, the dramatization of *Rebecca* was relatively straightforward; indeed, it would have been foolish to tamper with the irresistible thrust of Miss du Maurier's narrative. *Breeze Anstey*, on the other hand, demanded an almost complete reworking of the source material. A year or so after *Country Matters* had been screened, Derek Granger described the process of dramatization to a group of Granada trainees:

> If you read *Breeze Anstey* and then see it, I think the film version seems very close, and so, in fact, it is in atmosphere and feeling. Almost every detail of the story makes its point somewhere in the script and the dialogue is very close to the original. But the likeness is rather deceptive because the making of the script involved Whitemore in a radical reworking. Until about two-thirds of the way in, almost none of the incidents in the script (although most of them are preserved) occur in the same sequence as the original. The building of a strong dramatic curve made it necessary for Whitemore to really unpick the story, almost paragraph by paragraph, and then put it back together again in its most telling dramatic sequence.

This is what makes the business of adaptation so exciting and rewarding for the writer. One is not merely translating a story on the page into a story on the screen; one is creating something new—a film or play, based on the original material, but with a life and vigour all of its own. Such a goal is possible, anyway, even if it is not always achieved (and sometimes, alas, not even attempted).

When the draft script is finished, the collaboration between writer and director usually begins. Let me clarify the distinction between a producer and a director. In television, a producer is generally in overall charge of a number of plays or a drama series; it is he who hires the writers, establishes the budgets, assigns directors and is ultimately responsible for the projects being realized. The director is the person who works with the actors, briefs the designer, decides how the play shall be shot and finally edits the whole thing. In other words, the director commands all the creative elements, while the producer occupies an executive role, making sure that everything runs smoothly. The degree of creative involvement a producer permits himself varies enormously from individual to individual; and as far as *Breeze Anstey* was concerned, Derek Granger exerted a powerful influence on all aspects of the production, examining every detail with tireless energy—'I read half a dozen books by Rosamund Lehmann to check period speech nuances,' he recalls, 'a nice fanatical exercise.'

In fact, Granger enjoyed a far closer collaboration with the director, Peter Wood, than I did. This was because the pressures of television scheduling meant that by the time *Breeze Anstey* was in production, I was already preparing to write another script for the *Country Matters* series and was thus unable to work with the unit on location. Nevertheless, Granger, Wood and I discussed the script in great detail, and, as a result of these tripartite meetings, several telling changes were made. For example, I had scripted that Lorn and Breeze should be music lovers, and that records played on their old gramophone should provide a musical background to some of the rural sequences. I had suggested Delius or Vaughan Williams. Peter Wood felt that this was too obviously creating a 'poetic' mood and argued that the music should be Cole Porter or other popular songs of the 1930s. Derek Granger supported this idea, reminding us of Noel Coward's dictum about the potency of cheap music. As it happened, his choice of music proved to be one of the most important elements in the finished film, reflecting Breeze's vulnerability and yearning for love in a most touching and effective manner.

Creative collaboration between writer and director lies at the heart of any successful dramatic enterprise, be it in the theatre, on film or on television. Arguments may rage furiously, but the lines of communication should always be kept open. And since the few short weeks of rehearsal speed past all too quickly, frankness is invariably the best policy—even though it is not always welcome. I remember discussing a script with Donald McWhinnie: 'I'm rather pleased with scene 20,' I said. 'Are you?' said McWhinnie, a master of taciturnity. 'I don't care for it at all.' So startled was I by his frankness that I immediately re-examined the scene and found that it was indeed badly flawed—and lost no time in revising it. McWhinnie's directness of approach is greatly to be preferred to that of some of his colleagues, who wait until *after* a performance before they opine: 'It's never worked properly that scene, has it?'

A director's influence can range from suggesting a new approach to entire sequences to small touches of imagination that, although barely noticed by an audience, add a convincing richness of texture to the finished production. As an example of this latter, let me quote a characteristic detail devised by Simon Langton for *Rebecca*. The sequence was short and relatively unimportant: a car was seen driving up to Maxim de Winter's house, Manderley. Two people, Maxim's sister and brother-in-law, got out of the car and went indoors. There was no dialogue; there were no specific stage directions. But Langton gave life to the scene by adding a small and subtle vignette: as Robert, the footman, emerged from the house to open the car door, he was hastily pulling on his jacket. This simple, apparently casual action gave Robert an off-stage life—it created a feeling of verisimilitude and, at the same time, it underlined the fact that Maxim's visitors had arrived early. Such brief moments are worth a dozen lines of dialogue, and it is a foolish writer who fails to realize that.

The extent to which a writer and director are able to collaborate depends largely on the internal structure of the television company for which they are working. Generally speaking, the traditional, compartmentalized method is preferred: the producer commissions the writer; the writer writes the script, which is then submitted to the director and finally realized by the actors and camera crews. This means that the writer works alone, and that any collaboration between him and the director is essentially one of interpretation. And yet in my experience the quality of the finished production is greatly enhanced if the writer and director are brought together as early as possible—preferably before the script is even drafted. Although this fact is commonly recognized within the television industry, few drama executives have shown any inclination to act upon it. As in the Civil Service, old habits die hard. Fortunately, there are occasional, enlightened exceptions: Charles Denton, the programme controller of ATV, made it possible for Franc Roddam and me to collaborate at all stages of the production of the drama/documentary *Dummy*; simi-

larly, Gerald Savory, when he was Head of BBC Plays, encouraged
Claude Whatham and me to work closely together throughout the
making of our film version of *Cider with Rosie*. It is, I think, no
accident that these two unusually close collaborations resulted in programmes that received the highest critical and popular acclaim.

In the case of a book like *Cider with Rosie*, in which narrative is secondary to the author's use of language and his delicate evocation of
remembered moods and emotions, the dramatist's task becomes difficult to define. Conventional play-writing techniques are worse than
useless; the screen writer's job must be to find equivalents for the
author's rich texture of verbal imagery, to create a counterpoint of
pictures and spoken words that suggests the atmosphere and inten-
tions of the original. And without frequent consultations between
writer and director, such a process would be impossible. However,
thanks to Gerald Savory's understanding of this problem, Whatham
and I were able to discuss the structure of the book, to look at the lo-
cations and to draft a rough outline of the script *before* I started
writing. And by this time, we were both thinking of *Cider with Rosie*
in terms of a film to be made rather than of a book to be adapted;
indeed, I suspect that we were thinking of it as 'our' *Cider with
Rosie*—an attitude that must have infuriated Laurie Lee, who
watched us with understandable anxiety as we filmed in and around
the little village of Slad.

Alas, I can offer no insight into the thoughts or opinions of those
whose work has been dramatized by the likes of me. Cravenly, I have
always excused myself from any proposed meetings, believing (and I
think justifiably) that an author's view of his own work can often be
curiously misleading. Furthermore, I have heard that such encoun-
ters are sometimes far from pleasant. There was, I am told, an
occasion when Giles Cooper, who was about to embark on the dramatization of Evelyn Waugh's *Men at Arms* trilogy, was taken to the
Hyde Park Hotel to meet the great man himself. To Cooper's delight,
the conversation proceeded with surprising cordiality; but pleasure
turned to alarm as it became increasingly clear that Waugh was under
the misapprehension that Cooper was the actor chosen to play the
leading role, Guy Crouchback—indeed, he congratulated the
producer, Michael Bakewell, on making such an excellent choice.
When the situation was finally clarified, Waugh responded with formidable hostility, saying that no dramatist was required: his novels
contained all the necessary scenes and dialogue, and that all the BBC

had to do was to follow what he had written. It would have taken a brave man to contradict him; and even greater courage would have been required to speak the simple truth—that novelists are seldom the best people to dramatize their own books. Partly, of course, this is a question of technique: dialogue that succeeds on the page rarely works when spoken. (And vice versa: one has only to glance at a page of an Alan Ayckbourn comedy to see how flat the dialogue looks— and yet how brilliantly it plays in the theatre.) But more important than technique is the manner in which the work has been conceived. When an author has spent many months writing a novel, it is, I suggest, almost impossible for him to re-think the material in dramatic form. Understandably, he will be reluctant to change the overall construction—often a vital process in dramatization—and will tend to cling to favourite passages in the book simply because of their literary merit. What a skilled adaptor can offer is the ruthlessness of objective appraisal. This was made very clear to me when I was asked to transform my stage play *Stevie* into a film; no matter how hard I tried, I was quite unable to think of the script in a new form. Obstinately, it remained a film version of a piece conceived and written for the theatre.

One further digression: it is, I regret to say, unnecessary for me to point out that all the productions I have mentioned, from *Cider with Rosie* to *Rebecca*, were written within the conventions of television naturalism. Perhaps this is not surprising; television drama tends to be exclusively naturalistic, after all. And yet there was a time, not so very long ago, when I looked forward to exploring a new and entirely televisual means of dramatic expression. In 1963 I wrote in the British Film Institute's now defunct television quarterly, *Contrast*.

> more of an effort should be made to discover and to define the medium's own dramatic language. There must surely exist, within television, ways and means of expressing ideas and emotions with a new clarity and directness.

Shortly afterwards, Troy Kennedy Martin expressed similar sentiments in the magazine, *Encore*:

> The deep-rooted attitude shared by artists, critics and executives within the industry alike that naturalism is synonymous with TV drama must be got rid of.

He then went on to define this new dramatic form:

> It will be much more personal in style. It will compress information, emphasize fluidity, free the camera from photographing faces and free the structure from the naturalist tyranny of time. Through stream-of-consciousness and diary form it will lead to interior thought, interior characterization. Further, it will open up 250 years of novels and stories from Defoe to Virginia Woolf, allowing television to draw ideas from a mainstream of English creative life rather than from a naturalist backwater.

And around the time that these brave words were written there was, briefly, a flowering of true originality in television drama—the remarkable Teletale series, for example, and the first season of Wednesday Plays (both these ventures, by the way, masterminded by one of the very few innovators of British television, James MacTaggart). Suddenly, there was a flutter of excitement; and young writers—and I was one, then—really believed that they were standing on the brink of something new and challenging.

But within two or three years, all this had died. Its demise can be blamed almost entirely on a shift of creative fashion. In the mid 1960s, the makers of television drama discovered Film; Kenneth Loach made a stunning debut as one of the Wednesday Play directors, and everyone was dazzled by the skill with which he created the illusion of documentary-like realism. A trend had been fabricated, and everyone jostled to follow it. Writers and directors yearned to make films, and the possibilities offered by televisual, non-naturalistic drama were quickly forgotten. It is, I suppose, possible that the constraints of naturalism will one day be broken, but I rather doubt it. Any attempt to seek a new way of expressing ideas in television drama is almost certain to be met with violent and vitriolic opposition—if not from programme executives, then from the columnists who label themselves as television critics. One has only to recall the reception that greeted Lindsay Anderson's production of *The Old Crowd* by Alan Bennett. The play may have been flawed, but at least Anderson and Bennett had the courage to explore their theme with an originality and an intelligence that are all too rare in any dramatic medium. Reject those qualities, and you condemn television drama to an eternity of bland and predictable mediocrity. Since David Mercer's untimely death, there has been only one author, Dennis Potter, who has stubbornly and consistently managed to push TV drama beyond these miserable boundaries—and even he, now, seems to work exclusively on film. Spiralling production costs and the constant battle for ratings make it extremely unlikely that any attempt will be made to revitalize the original television play; but it is still possible that someone will be brave enough to develop the craft of dramatization in a truly creative and televisual way. Of course, this does not mean that I am advocating that all conventional drama should be swept aside; it means merely that those of us involved in the making of television plays should be constantly aware that there may be alternative (and better) ways of expressing ourselves.

Let me conclude, as I began, with an example from my own experience. A few years ago, I wrote a television version of Helene Hanff's book *84 Charing Cross Road*, which had been sent to me by Mark Shivas, who was then working at the BBC. Miss Hanff's book is a collection of letters exchanged between an American writer (Miss Hanff herself) and a bookseller in London—at first glance, not ideal material for a television play. Shivas and I agreed that the letters should remain intact and that my task as adaptor would be to place them in some sort of dramatic context. Consequently, I invented a series of visual 'situations'—either in Miss Hanff's New York apartment or in and around the Charing Cross Road bookshop—which were interspersed with newsreel extracts and popular songs, indicating the passage of time (the correspondence lasted from 1949 to 1969). The letters were read over the visual 'situations', which were all fairly simple and self-explanatory, thus needing no additional dialogue to reinforce them. The entire production was studio-based. It was neither a conventional television play nor a documentary; it did not pretend to be a film, and it could not have worked in the theatre—and yet it contained vivid characterizations and expressed deep emotions. It was essentially, idiosyncratically, a television programme. It was also extremely popular. Who could ask for anything more?*

---

*Since writing this, *84 Charing Cross Road* has been produced most successfully in the theatre; which only goes to show that if the original text is good enough, it can be made to work in any medium.